Better Homes and Gardens®

italian
all-time
favorites

Better Homes and Gardens®

italian
all-time
favorites

WILEY

John Wiley & Sons, Inc.

John Wiley & Sons, Inc.
Publisher: Natalie Chapman
Associate Publisher: Jessica Goodman
Executive Editor: Anne Ficklen
Production Manager: Michael Olivo
Production Editor: Abby Saul
Cover Design: Suzanne Sunwoo
Art Director: Tai Blanche
Layout: Indianapolis Composition
  Services
Manufacturing Manager: Tom Hyland

Test Kitchen

Our seal assures you that every recipe in *Italian All-Time Favorites* has been tested in the Better Homes and Gardens® Test Kitchen. This means that each recipe is practical and reliable and meets our high standards of taste appeal. We guarantee your satisfaction with this book for as long as you own it.

This book is printed on acid-free paper.

For general information on our other products and services or for technical support, please contact our Customer Care Department within the United States at (877) 762–2974, outside the United States at (317) 572–3993 or fax (317) 572–4002.

Wiley also publishes its books in a variety of electronic formats. Some content that appears in print may not be available in electronic books. For more information about Wiley products, visit our web site at www.wiley.com.

Library of Congress Cataloging-in-Publication Data is available upon request.

ISBN: 978-1-4351-2633-6

Printed in China.

10 9 8 7 6 5 4 3 2 1

contents

appetizers

Asiago-Artichoke Dip, *page 30*

toasted RAVIOLI

Prep: 25 minutes
Cook: 45 minutes
Makes: 12 to 14 appetizers

¼ cup finely chopped onion

1 clove garlic, minced

1 tablespoon olive oil
   or butter

2 pounds tomatoes, peeled,
   seeded, and chopped

2 tablespoons snipped fresh
   basil, or 1 teaspoon
   dried basil, crushed

½ teaspoon salt

⅛ teaspoon ground black
   pepper

2 tablespoons tomato paste

1 egg, lightly beaten

2 tablespoons milk

1 16- to 20-ounce package
   frozen meat-filled
   ravioli, thawed

⅔ to 1 cup seasoned fine
   dry bread crumbs

   Cooking oil for deep-fat
   frying

   Grated Parmesan cheese
   (optional)

1 For sauce, in a medium saucepan, cook onion and garlic in hot olive oil or butter till onion is tender. Stir in tomatoes, dried basil (if using), salt, and pepper. Cover; cook over medium heat for about 10 minutes or till tomatoes are soft, stirring occasionally.

2 Uncover and stir in tomato paste. Bring to boiling; reduce heat. Simmer, uncovered, for about 20 minutes or till mixture reaches desired consistency, stirring occasionally. Stir in fresh basil, if using. Cover sauce; keep warm.

3 Meanwhile, in a small bowl, beat together egg and milk. Dip each ravioli in egg mixture; then dip in bread crumbs to coat.

4 In a heavy 3-quart saucepan, heat 2 inches of cooking oil to 350°F. Fry ravioli, a few at a time, in hot oil for about 2 minutes or till golden brown, turning once. Drain on paper towels. Keep warm in a 300°F oven while frying the rest.

5 To serve, sprinkle ravioli with Parmesan cheese, if you like. Serve with warm sauce for dipping.

Nutrition facts per serving: 222 cal., 13 g total fat (1 g sat. fat), 47 mg chol., 429 mg sodium, 19 g carb., 8 g protein.

meatball SLIDERS

Prep: 10 minutes
Cook: 4 to 5 hours (low)
or 2 to 2½ hours
(high)
Makes: 24 sliders

1 **large red onion, cut into thin wedges (1½ cups)**

2 **12-ounce packages frozen cooked Italian meatballs (24)**

1 **24- to 26-ounce jar marinara or pasta sauce (about 2¼ cups)**

1 **tablespoon balsamic vinegar**

½ **teaspoon crushed red pepper**

6 **slices provolone cheese, quartered (6 ounces)**

4 **roma tomatoes, sliced**

24 **cocktail buns, split, toasted if desired**

1 Place onion wedges in a 3½- or 4-quart slow cooker. Top with frozen meatballs. In a medium bowl, combine marinara sauce, balsamic vinegar, and crushed red pepper. Pour over meatballs.

2 Cover and cook on low-heat setting for 4 to 5 hours or on high-heat setting for 2 to 2½ hours.

3 Gently stir mixture in cooker. Place a cheese and a tomato slice on the bottom of each cocktail bun. Top each with a meatball; replace bun tops.

Nutrition facts per slider: 217 cal., 11 g total fat (5 g sat. fat), 24 mg chol., 516 mg sodium, 20 g carb., 10 g protein.

fontina-stuffed
MEATBALL KABOBS

Prep: 30 minutes
Grill: 10 minutes
Makes: 16 kabobs

1 egg, lightly beaten
⅓ cup grated Parmesan
  cheese
2 cloves garlic, minced
1 teaspoon dried Italian
  seasoning
½ teaspoon salt
⅛ teaspoon ground
  black pepper
1½ pounds lean ground beef
2 ounces thinly sliced
  prosciutto, chopped
16 ½-inch Fontina cheese
  cubes (1½ ounces)
8 canned artichoke hearts,
  drained and halved
1 6- to 8-ounce package
  fresh cremini
  mushrooms**
1 pint grape tomatoes
  Balsamic Glaze*
  Fresh basil (optional)

1 Combine egg, Parmesan, garlic, Italian seasoning, salt, and pepper. Add beef and prosciutto; mix well. Divide in 16 portions; shape around cheese cubes. On sixteen 8- to 10-inch skewers, thread meatballs, artichokes, mushrooms, and tomatoes, leaving ¼ inch between. Prepare Balsamic Glaze.

2 On charcoal grill, place kabobs on greased rack of grill directly over medium coals. Grill for 10 to 12 minutes or until meat is no longer pink (160°F), turning and brushing with half the glaze halfway through. To serve, drizzle with remaining glaze; sprinkle with fresh basil, if desired.

*__Balsamic Glaze:__ In a small saucepan, combine ⅓ cup balsamic vinegar; 2 teaspoons olive oil; 1 clove garlic, minced; ¼ teaspoon salt; ¼ teaspoon dried Italian seasoning; and ⅛ teaspoon black pepper. Bring to boiling; reduce heat. Simmer, uncovered, for 4 minutes or until reduced to about ¼ cup. Divide in half.

Nutrition facts per kabob: 269 cal., 15 g total fat (5 g sat. fat), 91 mg chol., 673 mg sodium, 8 g carb., 24 g protein.

**Note: To easily skewer mushrooms, pour boiling water over them to soften; drain.

supreme PIZZA FONDUE

This fun appetizer is a bit like deconstructed pizza. All of the elements are there—sausage, sauce, mushrooms, veggies, plus bread and cheese cubes for dipping.

Prep: 20 minutes
Cook: 15 minutes
Makes: 16 (¼-cup) servings

- **4 ounces bulk Italian sausage**
- **1 small onion, finely chopped (⅓ cup)**
- **1 clove garlic, minced**
- **1 26-ounce jar tomato pasta sauce**
- **1 cup chopped fresh mushrooms**
- **⅔ cup chopped pepperoni or Canadian-style bacon**
- **1 teaspoon dried basil or oregano**
- **½ cup chopped pitted black olives (optional)**
- **¼ cup finely chopped green sweet pepper (optional)**
- **Italian flatbread (focaccia) or Italian bread cubes, cooked tortellini, and/or mozzarella or provolone cheese cubes, for serving**

1 In large skillet, cook sausage, onion, and garlic over medium heat until meat is brown. Drain off fat.

2 Add pasta sauce, mushrooms, pepperoni, and basil. Bring to a boil; reduce heat. Cover and simmer for 10 minutes. If desired, stir in olives and green pepper. Cover and cook for 5 minutes more or until pepper is tender. Serve with bread cubes, tortellini, and/or cheese cubes for dipping.

Nutrition facts per serving: 80 cal., 5 g total fat (2 g sat. fat), 11 mg chol., 361 mg sodium, 7 g carb., 3 g protein.

Slow Cooker Directions: Prepare through step 1 as above. In a 3½- or 4-quart slow cooker, combine pasta sauce, mushrooms, pepperoni, and basil. Stir in the sausage mixture. Cover slow cooker; cook on low-heat setting for 3 hours. If desired, stir in olives and green pepper. Cover; cook on low-heat setting for 15 minutes more. Serve as above.

italian GRINDER DIP

Prep: 25 minutes
Cook: 4 to 5 hours (low)
    or 2 to 2½ hours
    (high)
Makes: 22 (about
    3-tablespoon)
    servings

1 **pound ground beef**

1 **pound bulk Italian
    sausage**

1 **cup chopped onion
    (1 large)**

3 **cloves garlic, minced**

¾ **cup chopped green sweet
    pepper (1 medium)**

1 **4-ounce can (drained
    weight) sliced
    mushrooms, drained**

1 **teaspoon fennel seeds,
    crushed**

1 **teaspoon dried oregano,
    crushed**

1 **teaspoon dried basil,
    crushed**

½ **teaspoon crushed red
    pepper**

1 **14- or 15-ounce can pizza
    sauce**

   **Sliced garlic bread and/or
    ciabatta bread, toasted**

   **Shredded mozzarella
    cheese**

1 In a large skillet, cook ground beef, sausage, onion, and garlic over medium-high heat until meat is brown, using a wooden spoon to break up meat as it cooks. Drain off fat.

2 In a 3½- or 4-quart slow cooker, combine meat mixture, sweet pepper, mushrooms, fennel seeds, oregano, basil, and crushed red pepper. Stir in pizza sauce.

3 Cover and cook on low-heat setting for 4 to 5 hours or on high-heat setting for 2 to 2½ hours. Serve on toasted bread; top with cheese.

Nutrition facts per serving: 148 cal., 12 g total fat (4 g sat. fat), 32 mg chol., 217 mg sodium, 3 g carb., 7 g protein.

sausage-mushroom
PIZZA POCKETS

These individual-size pastries make ideal treats for family parties or bowl-game gatherings as they appeal to both kids and adults.

Prep: 35 minutes
Bake: 12 minutes
Oven: 425°F
Makes: 24 pockets

8 ounces bulk hot or mild
   Italian sausage

¾ cup chopped fresh
   mushrooms

½ of an 8-ounce package
   cream cheese, softened

¼ cup finely shredded or
   grated Parmesan cheese

2 13.8-ounce packages
   refrigerated pizza dough
   (2 crusts)

1 egg, lightly beaten

1 tablespoon water

   Finely shredded or
   grated Parmesan cheese
   (optional)

   Pizza sauce, warmed
   (optional)

1 In a medium skillet, cook sausage and mushrooms until sausage is brown, breaking up sausage with a wooden spoon as it cooks. Drain off fat; cool slightly.

2 In a medium bowl, stir together cream cheese and the ¼ cup Parmesan cheese. Stir in sausage mixture.

3 Preheat oven to 425°F. Lightly grease two large baking sheets. On a lightly floured surface, unroll each package of pizza dough. If necessary, gently stretch each dough piece into a 12x9-inch rectangle. Using a sharp knife or pizza cutter, cut each rectangle into twelve 3-inch squares. Place about 1 tablespoon of the sausage-cheese mixture in the center of each square. Fold dough over sausage-cheese mixture, forming triangles. Press the triangle edges with the tines of a fork to seal. Place the triangle pockets on the prepared baking sheets. Prick each top a few times with the fork tines.

4 In a small bowl, stir together egg and water. Brush tops of pockets with egg mixture, and if desired, sprinkle with additional Parmesan cheese. Bake for about 12 minutes or until pockets are golden. Serve warm. If desired, serve with pizza sauce.

Nutrition facts per pocket: 124 cal., 6 g total fat (2 g sat. fat), 22 mg chol., 205 mg sodium, 12 g carb., 4 g protein.

italian CHICKEN SPIRALS

These colorful spirals are filled with green spinach, pink prosciutto, and a white cheese spread.

Prep: 35 minutes
Bake: 25 minutes
Oven: 375°F
Makes: 36 appetizers

- 6 **large skinless, boneless chicken breast halves (about 2 pounds total)**
- 6 **medium spinach leaves, stems removed**
- 6 **thin slices prosciutto (about 2½ ounces total)**
- ½ **cup mascarpone cheese or cream cheese, softened**
- 1 **tablespoon olive oil**
- ¼ **teaspoon paprika**
- ¾ **cup mayonnaise**
- ½ **cup loosely packed fresh basil**
- ½ **small shallot**
- ½ **clove garlic**
  Basil Mayonnaise*

1 Preheat oven to 375°F. Place a chicken breast half between 2 pieces of plastic wrap. Pound chicken lightly to ¼-inch thickness. Repeat with remaining chicken breast halves. Set aside.

2 Place spinach leaves in a colander set in sink; pour boiling water over leaves. Drain on paper towels.

3 Place a chicken breast half, smooth side down, on a cutting board or other flat surface. Season with salt and pepper. Arrange prosciutto on chicken. Spread a rounded tablespoon of cheese evenly over prosciutto. Arrange a spinach leaf on top.

4 Roll chicken tightly from one long edge and place, seam side down, in a greased shallow baking pan. Repeat with remaining chicken breast halves. Combine olive oil and paprika; brush over chicken.

5 Bake for 25 to 30 minutes or until chicken is tender and no longer pink; cool slightly. Cover and refrigerate for several hours.

6 To serve, trim off ends of chicken rolls. Cut each chicken roll into 6 slices. Arrange slices on serving plate. Serve with Basil Mayonnaise and garnish with fresh basil, if desired.

*Basil Mayonnaise: Combine mayonnaise, fresh basil, shallot, and garlic in a food processor bowl or blender container. Cover and process or blend until almost smooth. Cover and chill for up to 4 hours.

Nutrition facts per serving: 84 cal., 7 g total fat (2 g sat. fat), 20 mg chol., 75 mg sodium, 0 g carb., 6 g protein.

Make-Ahead Directions: Prepare chicken. Cover and chill for up to 8 hours. Prepare mayonnaise. Cover and chill for up to 4 hours.

parmesan-crusted
CHICKEN NUGGETS

Prep: 20 minutes
Bake: 10 minutes
Oven: 425°F
Makes: about 40 servings

1¼ **pounds skinless, boneless chicken breasts**

2 **egg whites**

1 **cup finely shredded Parmigiano-Reggiano cheese or Parmesan cheese (4 ounces)**

1 **cup panko (Japanese-style) bread crumbs**

¼ **teaspoon ground black pepper**

Nonstick cooking spray

1 **cup purchased marinara sauce**

1 Preheat oven to 425°F. Line a large baking sheet with parchment paper or foil; set aside. Cut chicken into 1-inch pieces.

2 In a medium bowl, whisk egg whites until frothy. In another medium bowl, combine cheese, bread crumbs, and pepper.

3 Add chicken to egg whites; toss gently to coat. Transfer chicken, a few pieces at a time, to cheese mixture; toss gently to coat (if necessary, press lightly to adhere). Place chicken, without touching, on the prepared baking sheet. Lightly coat chicken with nonstick cooking spray.

4 Bake, uncovered, for 10 to 15 minutes or until chicken is no longer pink and coating is lightly browned. Meanwhile, heat marinara sauce. Serve marinara sauce with chicken for dipping.

Nutrition facts per serving: 34 cal., 1 g total fat (0 g sat. fat), 10 mg chol., 77 mg sodium, 2 g carb., 5 g protein.

antipasti PLATTER

Start to Finish: 30 minutes
Makes: 12 servings

1 pound assorted sliced deli meats (such as salami, spicy capocollo, prosciutto, and/or mortadella)

8 ounces assorted cheeses, cubed (such as Parmesan, Asiago, fresh mozzarella, provolone, and/or blue cheese)

1½ cups purchased marinated olives and/or marinated artichoke hearts

1 12-ounce jar roasted red and/or yellow sweet peppers, drained and cut into ½-inch-wide strips

1 cup cherry and/or grape tomatoes

Snipped fresh basil (optional)

½ cup olive oil

¼ teaspoon coarse kosher salt

¼ teaspoon ground black pepper

1 8-ounce loaf Italian bread, sliced

Arrange meats, cheeses, olives, sweet peppers, and tomatoes on a large platter. If desired, sprinkle with fresh basil. Place oil in a shallow bowl or dish. Sprinkle with salt and pepper. Drizzle some of the oil mixture over the meats, cheeses, and vegetables. Serve remaining oil mixture beside tray for dipping or drizzling. Serve with bread.

Nutrition facts per serving: 363 cal., 27 g total fat (8 g sat. fat), 46 mg chol., 1100 mg sodium, 14 g carb., 17 g protein.

pesto SHRIMP CAPRESE SKEWERS

Known as bocconcini, the small fresh mozzarella balls featured in this recipe represent Italy on a stick when paired with shrimp and tomatoes brushed with pesto.

Prep: 30 minutes
Chill: 1 hour
Makes: 20 skewers

- 20 **fresh or frozen medium shrimp**
- 1 **tablespoon olive oil**
- ¼ **cup purchased basil pesto**
- 20 **bocconcini or 1-inch chunks fresh mozzarella cheese**
- 20 **grape tomatoes**
  Purchased basil pesto
- 2 **tablespoons bottled balsamic vinaigrette dressing**
  Ground black pepper (optional)

1 Thaw shrimp, if frozen. Peel and devein shrimp, leaving tails intact. Rinse shrimp and pat dry with paper towels.

2 In a large skillet, cook shrimp in hot oil over medium heat for 2 to 4 minutes or until opaque. Spread shrimp in a single layer on a baking sheet; cover and chill for at least 1 hour. In a medium bowl, combine shrimp and the ¼ cup pesto; toss to coat.

3 On each of twenty 4-inch skewers, thread a shrimp, a bocconcini, and a tomato. Serve immediately or cover and chill for up to 4 hours. To serve, brush with additional pesto and balsamic vinaigrette. If desired, sprinkle with pepper.

Nutrition facts per skewer: 125 cal., 9 g total fat (5 g sat. fat), 47 mg chol., 156 mg sodium, 1 g carb., 9 g protein.

Make-Ahead Directions: Cover and chill cooked shrimp and pesto mixture for up to 24 hours before serving. Thread onto skewers as directed.

italian-style WONTONS

Prep: 35 minutes
Cook: 1 minute per batch
Oven: 300°F
Makes: 24 wontons

½ **cup finely shredded mozzarella cheese (2 ounces)**

¼ **cup snipped fresh basil**

¼ **cup chopped walnuts**

3 **tablespoons oil-packed dried tomatoes, drained and finely chopped**

2 **tablespoons finely chopped pitted black olives**

1 **scallion, thinly sliced**

24 **square wonton wrappers**

Cooking oil or shortening for deep-fat frying

¾ **cup purchased marinara sauce (optional)**

1 Preheat oven to 300°F. For filling, in a small bowl stir together cheese, basil, walnuts, dried tomatoes, olives, and scallion.

2 For each wonton, place one wonton wrapper on a flat surface with one corner toward you. Spoon a rounded teaspoon of the filling just below the center of the wonton wrapper. Fold the bottom point over the filling and tuck it under the filling. Roll the wonton wrapper once to cover filling, leaving about 1 inch unrolled at the top of the wrapper. Moisten the right corner with water. Grasp right and left corners and bring them toward you below the filling. Overlap the left corner over the right corner. Press firmly to seal.

3 Pour 2 inches of oil into a heavy saucepan or deep-fat fryer; heat to 365°F. Fry wontons, a few at a time, for 1 to 2½ minutes or until golden brown. Drain on paper towels. Keep warm in oven while frying the remaining wontons. If desired, serve with heated marinara sauce for dipping.

Nutrition facts per wonton: 55 cal., 4 g total fat (1 g sat. fat), 2 mg chol., 41 mg sodium, 4 g carb., 1 g protein.

caponata

A classic eggplant relish from Sicily, caponata is a combination of sweet and sour flavors lent by a blend of balsamic vinegar and capers.

Prep: 20 minutes
Cook: 35 minutes
Makes: 48 (1-tablespoon) servings (3 cups)

- 3 tablespoons olive oil
- 1 cup chopped onion
- 2 large cloves garlic, minced
- 8 ounces fresh mushrooms, chopped
- 3 cups diced eggplant
- 3 tablespoons balsamic vinegar
- 1 14.5-ounce can whole tomatoes, undrained
- 2 tablespoons capers, drained
- 2 teaspoons sugar
- ½ teaspoon salt
- ¼ teaspoon dried thyme, crushed
- ⅛ teaspoon crushed red pepper
- Toasted semolina bread

1 Heat 1 tablespoon of the oil in a large skillet over medium heat. Add the onion and garlic and cook for 4 to 5 minutes, until softened.

2 Add another tablespoon of oil and the mushrooms to the pan and increase the heat to medium-high. Cook vegetables, stirring occasionally, for 6 to 8 minutes or until mushrooms are tender. Add the remaining 1 tablespoon oil and the eggplant to the skillet, then cover and cook for 6 minutes more.

3 Add the vinegar and continue to cook uncovered, stirring, until evaporated. Add the tomatoes and their liquid, breaking up the tomatoes with a spoon. Stir in the capers, sugar, salt, thyme, and crushed red pepper. Simmer for 15 to 20 minutes or until eggplant is completely tender and mixture is thick.

4 Transfer mixture to a food processor. Process, pulsing on and off 3 or 4 times, just until coarsely chopped. Transfer to a serving bowl. Spread on semolina bread.

Nutrition facts per serving: 15 cal., 1 g total fat (0 g sat. fat), 0 mg chol., 47 mg sodium, 1 g carb., 0 g protein.

marinated MUSHROOMS AND ARTICHOKES

Prep: 25 minutes
Marinate: 8 to 24 hours
Stand: 30 minutes
Makes: 8 servings

8 ounces small whole fresh cremini and/or button mushrooms

¾ cup water

2 tablespoons orange juice

2 large cloves garlic

½ teaspoon salt

¼ cup orange-flavor olive oil or olive oil*

¼ cup white wine vinegar

1 tablespoon snipped fresh oregano

2 teaspoons Dijon-style mustard

¼ teaspoon salt

1 8- or 9-ounce package frozen artichoke hearts, thawed and drained (if necessary)

1½ cups pitted green and/or black olives (such as Cerignola or Kalamata)

½ cup roasted red sweet pepper strips (optional)

① In a large saucepan, combine mushrooms, the water, juice, garlic, and ½ teaspoon salt. Bring to boiling; reduce heat. Simmer, covered, for 10 minutes. Drain; cool slightly.

② Meanwhile, for marinade, in a large bowl, whisk together oil, vinegar, oregano, mustard, and ¼ teaspoon salt. Add mushrooms, artichoke hearts, olives, and, if desired, roasted peppers; toss gently to coat. Cover and marinate in the refrigerator for 8 to 24 hours, stirring occasionally.

③ Let stand at room temperature for 30 minutes before serving. Use wooden toothpicks or skewers to serve.

Nutrition facts per serving: 126 cal., 11 g total fat (2 g sat. fat), 0 mg chol., 651 mg sodium, 6 g carb., 2 g protein.

*Tip: If using unflavored olive oil, add ½ teaspoon finely shredded orange peel to the marinade.

BALSAMIC cremini– topped FLATBREAD

Prep: 15 minutes
Grill: 5 minutes
Makes: 6 servings

- 2 **cups sliced fresh cremini mushrooms**
- 1 **tablespoon olive oil**
- ¼ **teaspoon salt**
- ¼ **teaspoon ground black pepper**
- 2 **tablespoons balsamic vinegar**
- 1 **10-inch prebaked packaged pizza crust**
- ⅓ **cup crumbled goat cheese (chèvre)**
- 1 **tablespoon snipped fresh marjoram**

1 In a large skillet, cook mushrooms in hot oil over medium heat until tender, stirring occasionally. Sprinkle with salt and pepper. Stir in vinegar. Cook, uncovered, until all of the vinegar is evaporated, stirring occasionally.

2 For a charcoal grill, grill prebaked pizza crust on the rack of uncovered grill directly over medium coals for about 3 minutes or until bottom is lightly browned. (For a gas grill, preheat grill. Reduce heat to medium. Place prebaked pizza crust on grill rack over heat. Cover and grill as above.) Remove from grill.

3 Spread cooked mushrooms over browned side of pizza crust. Sprinkle with cheese. Return pizza crust to grill. Cover and grill for 2 to 3 minutes more or until bottom is lightly browned and topping is heated through. Sprinkle with marjoram. To serve, cut into six wedges.

Nutrition facts per serving: 138 cal., 6 g total fat (2 g sat. fat), 7 mg chol., 220 mg sodium, 16 g carb., 4 g protein.

asiago-artichoke DIP

Prep: 30 minutes
Bake: 25 minutes
Oven: 350°F
Makes: 12 (¼-cup) servings

- 1 **14-ounce can artichoke hearts, rinsed and drained**
- 2 **ounces thinly sliced prosciutto**
- 1 **cup arugula, chopped**
- ½ **cup shredded Asiago cheese (2 ounces)**
- 2 **tablespoons all-purpose flour**
- 1 **8-ounce carton sour cream**
- ½ **cup mayonnaise**
- ½ **cup bottled roasted red sweet peppers, drained and finely chopped**
- ¼ **cup thinly sliced scallions (2)**
  Shredded Asiago cheese (optional)
  Thinly sliced scallions
  Crackers and/or toasted baguette slices

1 Preheat oven to 350°F. Squeeze artichokes to remove excess liquid. Coarsely chop artichokes. Set aside.

2 Stack prosciutto slices; cut crosswise into thin strips. Cut strips in half; separate pieces. In a medium skillet, cook and stir prosciutto over medium heat until brown and slightly crisp. Add arugula; cook and stir for 1 minute more.

3 In a large bowl, toss together ½ cup cheese and flour. Stir in sour cream, mayonnaise, roasted peppers, ¼ cup scallions, and arugula mixture. Transfer to an ungreased 9-inch pie plate. If desired, sprinkle with additional cheese.

4 Bake for about 25 minutes or until edge is bubbly and mixture is heated through. Sprinkle with additional scallions. Serve dip with crackers and/or baguette slices.

Nutrition facts per serving: 157 cal., 14 g total fat (5 g sat. fat), 18 mg chol., 312 mg sodium, 4 g carb., 4 g protein.

tomato AND MOZZARELLA TARTS

Prep: 20 minutes
Bake: 12 minutes
Oven: 400°F
Makes: 8 or 9 tarts

½ of a 17.3-ounce package frozen puff pastry sheets (1 sheet), thawed

1½ tablespoons finely shredded Parmesan cheese

3 ounces salted fresh mozzarella cheese, very thinly sliced (8 or 9 slices)

1 large roma tomato, thinly sliced (8 or 9 slices)

Salt and ground black pepper

Small fresh basil leaves

1 Preheat oven to 400°F. Line a baking sheet with parchment paper.

2 On a lightly floured surface, unfold pastry. Cut into 8 or 9 rounds with a 3-inch biscuit cutter. Place 1 inch apart on the prepared baking sheet. Using a fork, prick each round in several places. Bake for about 10 minutes or until puffed.

3 Sprinkle rounds with Parmesan cheese; top with mozzarella cheese and tomato slices. Sprinkle with salt and pepper.

4 Bake for 12 to 14 minutes or until pastry is golden brown. Sprinkle tarts with basil. Serve warm.

Nutrition facts per tart: 75 cal., 5 g total fat (2 g sat. fat), 8 mg chol., 207 mg sodium, 4 g carb., 3 g protein.

gorgonzola-pear
FOCACCIA

Gorgonzola always pairs well with fresh pears. Try them atop purchased Italian flatbread for an appetizer that's out of the ordinary and elegant.

Start to Finish: 25 minutes
Oven: 425°F
Makes: 12 to 16 servings

1 **12-inch Italian flatbread (focaccia), or one 1-pound Italian bread shell**

1 **medium pear, halved, cored, and very thinly sliced**

1 **small red onion, cut into thin wedges**

1 **tablespoon olive oil**

1 **cup crumbled Gorgonzola cheese (4 ounces)**

¼ **cup chopped toasted walnuts**

1 Preheat oven to 425°F. Place bread on an ungreased baking sheet or pizza pan. Arrange pear slices and onion wedges on top. Drizzle with olive oil. Sprinkle with Gorgonzola.

2 Bake for 10 minutes. Sprinkle with toasted walnuts. To serve, cut into wedges.

Nutrition facts per serving: 175 cal., 8 g total fat (2 g sat. fat), 10 mg chol., 364 mg sodium, 19 g carb., 7 g protein.

pesto-tomato BRUSCHETTA

Arugula adds a twist to the traditional Italian pine nut pesto.

Start to Finish: 40 minutes
Makes: 12 (2-slice) servings

Pine Nut Pesto*

24 ½-inch-thick slices
   baguette-style French
   bread, toasted, or whole
   grain crackers

 1 ounce Parmesan or
   Romano cheese, shaved

 1 cup red and/or yellow
   cherry tomatoes, halved
   or quartered, or 2 roma
   tomatoes, sliced

   **Fresh basil sprigs
   (optional)**

   **Pine nuts, chopped
   walnuts, or chopped
   almonds, toasted
   (optional)**

Spread Pine Nut Pesto onto baguette slices. Top with shaved Parmesan and tomatoes. If desired, top with basil and nuts.

***Pine Nut Pesto:** In a small food processor, combine 1 cup firmly packed fresh basil; 1 cup torn fresh arugula or spinach; ¼ cup grated Parmesan or Romano cheese; ¼ cup toasted pine nuts, chopped walnuts, or chopped almonds; 1 clove garlic, quartered; 1 tablespoon olive oil; 1 tablespoon white balsamic vinegar; and ¼ teaspoon salt. Cover and process with several on-off turns until a paste forms, stopping several times to scrape the sides. Process in enough water, 1 tablespoon at a time, until pesto reaches the consistency of soft butter.

Nutrition facts per serving: 89 cal., 3 g total fat (1 g sat. fat), 3 mg chol., 246 mg sodium, 11 g carb., 4 g protein.

Make-Ahead Directions: Toast bread slices and prepare Pine Nut Pesto as directed. Cover and chill for up to 24 hours. Serve as directed.

soups AND STEWS

Italian Wedding Soup, *page 42*

beef, ORZO, AND ESCAROLE SOUP

Orzo, sometimes called rosamarina, is a small, rice-shaped pasta. If orzo is not available, substitute spaghetti or linguine broken into ¼- to ½-inch-long pieces.

Prep: 5 minutes
Cook: 25 minutes
Makes: 4 servings

12 ounces lean ground beef

1 small fennel bulb, chopped (about ⅔ cup)

1 medium onion, chopped (about ½ cup)

2 cloves garlic, minced

4 cups beef broth

2 cups water

1 teaspoon dried oregano, crushed

2 bay leaves

¼ teaspoon cracked black pepper

½ cup orzo

4 cups shredded escarole, curly endive, and/or spinach

3 ounces Parmigiano-Reggiano or Parmesan cheese with rind, cut into 4 wedges (optional)

1 In a large saucepan, combine beef, fennel, onion, and garlic. Cook, uncovered, over medium-high heat for 5 minutes or until meat is browned and vegetables are nearly tender, stirring occasionally. Drain fat, if necessary.

2 Stir in broth, water, oregano, bay leaves, and pepper. Bring to boiling; reduce heat. Simmer, covered, for 10 minutes. Remove bay leaves; discard.

3 Add orzo. Return to boiling; reduce heat to medium. Boil gently, uncovered, for 10 minutes or until pasta is just tender, stirring occasionally. Remove from heat; stir in escarole.

4 To serve, place a wedge of cheese in each of four soup bowls, if desired, and ladle hot soup into bowls.

Nutrition facts per serving: 262 cal., 10 g total fat (4 g sat. fat), 54 mg chol., 873 mg sodium, 22 g carb., 21 g protein.

italian BEEF SOUP

Although pesto in a jar is a great convenience product, refrigerated pesto stays fresher and has better color. You'll get the best flavor from it, if you can find it.

Start to Finish: 25 minutes
Makes: 6 servings

1 **pound lean ground beef**

2 **14-ounce cans beef broth**

1 **16-ounce package frozen broccoli and/or cauliflower florets**

1 **14.5-ounce can diced tomatoes, undrained**

1 **5.5-ounce can tomato juice (¾ cup)**

1 **cup dried rotini, wagon wheel, or other small pasta**

½ **cup purchased basil pesto**

1 In a 4-quart Dutch oven, cook ground beef over medium heat until browned. Drain off fat.

2 Stir beef broth, broccoli, tomatoes, and tomato juice into meat mixture in saucepan. Bring to boiling; stir in pasta. Reduce heat. Simmer, covered, for about 10 minutes or until vegetables and pasta are tender. Stir in pesto and serve.

Nutrition facts per serving: 317 cal., 16 g total fat (5 g sat. fat), 54 mg chol., 905 mg sodium, 20 g carb., 21 g protein.

italian WEDDING SOUP

Orzo is a popular addition to many Italian soups. Dried tomatoes give the meatballs a pleasant tang.

Prep: 40 minutes
Cook: 10 minutes
Makes: 6 servings

- 1 **large onion**
- 3 **oil-packed dried tomatoes, finely chopped**
- 2 **teaspoons dried Italian seasoning, crushed**
- 1 **pound lean ground beef**
- 1 **egg, lightly beaten**
- ¼ **cup fine dry bread crumbs**
- ¼ **teaspoon salt**
- 2 **teaspoons olive oil**
- 1 **large fennel bulb**
- 4 **14-ounce cans chicken broth**
- 6 **cloves garlic, thinly sliced**
- ½ **teaspoon ground black pepper**
- ¾ **cup orzo**
- 5 **cups shredded fresh spinach**

1 Finely chop one-third of the onion; thinly slice remaining onion. In a large bowl, combine chopped onion, dried tomatoes, and 1 teaspoon of the Italian seasoning. Add ground beef, egg, bread crumbs, and salt; mix well. Shape into 12 meatballs. In a Dutch oven, brown meatballs in hot oil. Carefully drain off fat.

2 Meanwhile, cut off and discard upper stalks of fennel. If desired, save some of the feathery fennel leaves for a garnish. Remove any wilted outer layers; cut off a thin slice from fennel base. Cut fennel into thin wedges.

3 Add fennel, sliced onion, chicken broth, garlic, black pepper, and the remaining 1 teaspoon Italian seasoning to meatballs in Dutch oven. Bring to boiling; stir in uncooked orzo. Simmer, uncovered, for 10 to 15 minutes or until orzo is tender.

4 Stir in spinach. If desired, garnish soup with reserved fennel leaves.

Nutrition facts per serving: 292 cal., 11 g total fat (3 g sat. fat), 86 mg chol., 1352 mg sodium, 27 g carb., 20 g protein.

Slow Cooker Directions: Prepare as directed in step 1. After browning meatballs, place meatballs and sliced onion in a 5-quart slow cooker. Add fennel, broth, garlic, black pepper, and the remaining 1 teaspoon Italian seasoning. Cover and cook on low-heat setting for 8 to 10 hours or on high-heat setting for 4 to 5 hours. If using low-heat setting, turn cooker to high-heat setting. Gently stir orzo into soup. Cover and cook for 15 minutes more. Stir in spinach. If desired, garnish with reserved fennel leaves.

italian BUFFET STEW

Prep: 20 minutes
Cook: 9 to 10 hours (low)
or 4½ to 5 hours
(high)
Makes: 6 to 8 servings

2½ **pounds boneless beef
chuck roast**

2 **medium onions, cut into
1-inch chunks**

1 **large red sweet pepper,
cut into ¾-inch pieces**

1 **14-ounce jar marinara
sauce**

1 **teaspoon bottled minced
garlic (2 cloves)**

½ **teaspoon salt**

½ **teaspoon dried oregano,
crushed**

¼ **teaspoon ground black
pepper**

2 **medium zucchini, cut into
¾-inch chunks**

**Hot cooked spaghetti
(optional)**

1 Trim fat from roast. Cut roast into 1-inch cubes. In a 3½- or 4-quart slow cooker, layer beef, onions, and red sweet pepper. Stir in spaghetti sauce, garlic, salt, oregano, and black pepper. Cover and cook on low-heat setting for 9 to 10 hours or on high-heat setting for 4½ to 5 hours.

2 If cooking on low, turn cooker to high. Add zucchini; cover and cook for 15 minutes more. Serve over hot cooked spaghetti, if desired.

Nutrition facts per serving of stew: 350 cal., 15 g total fat (6 g sat. fat), 101 mg chol., 505 mg sodium, 20 g carb., 32 g protein.

chicken MINESTRONE SOUP

In Italy, there is no typical recipe for minestrone soup because it is prepared with any vegetables that happen to be available that day.

Start to Finish: 45 minutes
Makes: 8 servings

1 **cup sliced carrots
   (2 medium)**

½ **cup chopped celery
   (1 stalk)**

½ **cup chopped onion
   (1 medium)**

1 **tablespoon olive oil**

3 **14-ounce cans reduced-
   sodium chicken broth**

2 **15-ounce cans cannellini
   beans (white kidney
   beans), rinsed and drained**

8 **ounces skinless, boneless
   chicken breast halves, cut
   into bite-size pieces**

5 **ounces fresh green beans,
   cut into ½-inch pieces
   (1 cup), or frozen cut
   green beans**

¼ **teaspoon ground black
   pepper**

1 **cup bow-tie pasta**

1¼ **cups sliced halved zucchini
   and/or yellow summer
   squash**

1 **14.5-ounce can diced
   tomatoes with basil, garlic,
   and oregano, undrained**

   Snipped fresh oregano

   Ground black pepper

1 In a 5- to 6-quart Dutch oven, cook carrots, celery, and onion in hot oil over medium heat for 5 minutes, stirring occasionally.

2 Stir in broth, cannellini beans, chicken, green beans, and ¼ teaspoon pepper. Bring to boiling. Stir in pasta; reduce heat. Simmer, uncovered, for 5 minutes.

3 Stir in zucchini and/or yellow squash. Return to boiling; reduce heat. Simmer, uncovered, for 8 to 10 minutes more or until pasta is tender and green beans are crisp-tender. Stir in tomatoes; heat through. Sprinkle each serving with oregano and additional pepper.

Nutrition facts per serving: 173 cal., 3 g total fat (0 g sat. fat), 16 mg chol., 818 mg sodium, 27 g carb., 17 g protein.

parmesan-pesto
CHICKEN SOUP

This Italian version of chicken noodle soup makes an ideal dinner on a cold day. Bread topped with purchased pesto and Parmesan creates a hassle-free accompaniment.

Start to Finish: 30 minutes
Makes: 4 servings

- 2 **14-ounce cans reduced-sodium chicken broth**
- 1 **teaspoon dried Italian seasoning, crushed**
- 1 **teaspoon bottled minced garlic (2 cloves)**
- 12 **ounces skinless, boneless chicken breasts**
- ¾ **cup small shell macaroni**
- 2 **½-inch-thick slices Italian bread, halved crosswise**
- 2 **tablespoons purchased basil pesto**
- ¼ **cup finely shredded Parmesan cheese**
- ¾ **cup frozen shelled peas**
- 2 **medium scallions, thinly sliced (¼ cup)**

1 Combine broth, Italian seasoning, and garlic in a medium saucepan; bring to boiling.

2 Meanwhile, cut chicken into bite-size cubes. Add chicken and macaroni to broth. Return mixture to boiling; reduce heat. Simmer, uncovered, for 8 to 9 minutes or till pasta is tender and chicken is no longer pink, stirring occasionally.

3 Meanwhile, preheat broiler. Spread one side of each halved bread slice with pesto. Sprinkle with cheese. Place on broiler rack. Broil 3 to 4 inches from heat for 2 minutes or till cheese just begins to melt.

4 Add frozen peas and scallion to broth mixture; cook for 2 minutes more. Ladle into soup bowls. Top each serving with a slice of cheesy toasted bread.

Nutrition facts per serving: 329 cal., 9 g total fat (2 g sat. fat), 57 mg chol., 622 mg sodium, 29 g carb., 30 g protein.

chicken AND SHELLS SOUP

Start to Finish: 30 minutes
Makes: 4 servings

2 **14-ounce cans reduced-sodium chicken broth**

1 **teaspoon dried Italian seasoning, crushed**

½ **teaspoon bottled minced garlic (1 clove)**

12 **ounces skinless, boneless chicken breast halves, cut into bite-size pieces**

¾ **cup small shell macaroni**

¾ **cup frozen peas**

¼ **cup thinly sliced scallions (2)**

1 In a medium saucepan, combine chicken broth, Italian seasoning, and garlic; bring to boiling. Add chicken and pasta. Return to boiling; reduce heat. Simmer, uncovered, for 8 to 9 minutes or until pasta is tender and chicken is no longer pink, stirring occasionally.

2 Add peas and green onion; cook for about 2 minutes more or until peas are crisp-tender.

Nutrition facts per serving: 211 cal., 2 g total fat (0 g sat. fat), 49 mg chol., 546 mg sodium, 21 g carb., 27 g protein.

turkey-ravioli SOUP

Need a quick meal? This soup is a creative way to use leftover turkey. The ravioli is both unexpected and filling.

Start to Finish: 20 minutes
Makes: 6 servings

- 6 **cups reduced-sodium chicken broth**
- ¾ **cup chopped red sweet pepper (1 medium)**
- ½ **cup chopped onion (1 medium)**
- 1½ **teaspoons dried Italian seasoning, crushed**
- 1½ **cups cooked turkey cut into bite-size pieces (about 8 ounces)**
- 1 **9-ounce package refrigerated cheese ravioli**
- 2 **cups shredded fresh spinach**

   Finely shredded Parmesan cheese (optional)

Combine chicken broth, sweet pepper, onion, and Italian seasoning in a Dutch oven. Bring to boiling; reduce heat. Add turkey and ravioli. Return to boiling; reduce heat. Simmer, uncovered, for about 6 minutes or just until ravioli is tender. Stir in spinach. If desired, sprinkle with Parmesan cheese before serving.

Nutrition facts per serving: 228 cal., 5 g total fat (3 g sat. fat), 44 mg chol., 823 mg sodium, 24 g carb., 21 g protein.

Tip: To save time, chop the turkey while the onion mixture comes to a boil; shred the spinach while cooking the ravioli.

sausage-tortellini STEW

Prep: 10 minutes
Cook: 6 hours (low) or 3 hours (high)
Makes: 6 servings

4 **sweet Italian turkey sausage links, casings removed**

1 **28-ounce can crushed tomatoes with garlic, basil, and oregano**

1 **9-ounce package frozen cut green beans**

1 **large onion, chopped**

½ **teaspoon Italian seasoning**

1 **9-ounce package refrigerated cheese tortellini**

1 **tablespoon chopped fresh oregano**

1 **cup water**

1 Crumble sausages into a bowl and stir together with tomatoes, green beans, onion, and Italian seasoning; place mixture in slow cooker. Cover and cook for 3 hours on high or 6 hours on low.

2 When there are 20 minutes remaining, stir in tortellini, oregano and the 1 cup water; continue cooking. Serve immediately.

Nutrition facts per serving: 305 cal., 10 g total fat (2 g sat. fat), 57 mg chol., 709 mg sodium, 34 g carb., 19 g protein.

pizza SOUP

Start to Finish: 20 minutes
Makes: 6 servings

1 cup chopped onion

1 cup chopped green sweet
   pepper

1 cup sliced fresh
   mushrooms

1 cup sliced halved zucchini

1 14-ounce can beef broth

1 14.5-ounce can diced
   tomatoes with garlic,
   basil, and oregano,
   undrained

1 8-ounce can tomato sauce
   with garlic and onion

4 ounces cooked smoked
   turkey sausage, thinly
   sliced

½ teaspoon pizza seasoning

½ cup shredded reduced-fat
   mozzarella cheese
   (2 ounces)

1 In a medium saucepan, combine onion, sweet pepper, mushrooms, zucchini, and ¼ cup of the broth. Bring to boiling; reduce heat. Simmer, covered, for 5 minutes.

2 Stir in remaining broth, tomatoes, tomato sauce, sausage, and pizza seasoning. Simmer for 5 to 10 minutes more or until vegetables are tender. Top each serving with cheese.

Nutrition facts per serving: 119 cal., 3 g total fat (1 g sat. fat), 17 mg chol., 1018 mg sodium, 14 g carb., 9 g protein.

white BEAN SOUP WITH SAUSAGE AND KALE

Start to Finish: 30 minutes
Makes: 5 servings

12 ounces fresh, mild Italian sausage links, sliced ½ inch thick

¼ cup water

1 medium onion, chopped (½ cup)

1 teaspoon bottled minced garlic (2 cloves)

1 tablespoon cooking oil

2 15-ounce cans white kidney (cannellini) beans, rinsed and drained

2 14-ounce cans reduced-sodium chicken broth

1 14.5-ounce can diced tomatoes with garlic, basil, and oregano undrained

4 cups coarsely chopped kale or spinach

Ground black pepper

1 Combine sliced sausage and the ¼ cup water in a large skillet. Bring to boiling; reduce heat. Simmer, covered, for about 10 minutes or till sausage is no longer pink. Uncover and cook for about 5 minutes more or till sausage is browned, stirring frequently. Remove sausage with a slotted spoon; set aside.

2 Meanwhile, cook onion and garlic in hot oil in a large saucepan for about 5 minutes or till onion is tender. Stir in beans, broth, and tomatoes. Cover and bring to boiling; reduce heat. Simmer, covered, for 5 minutes.

3 Stir in cooked sausage and kale or spinach. Simmer, uncovered, for about 3 minutes more or until kale or spinach is tender. Season to taste with pepper.

Nutrition facts per serving: 394 cal., 19 g total fat (7 g sat. fat), 46 mg chol., 1510 mg sodium, 38 g carb., 25 g protein.

pasta FAGIOLI

Prep: 20 minutes
Cook: 20 minutes
Makes: 6 servings

- 1 **cup chopped onion
  (1 large)**
- 3 **ounces pancetta or bacon,
  chopped**
- 3 **cloves garlic, thinly sliced**
- 1 **tablespoon olive oil**
- ¾ **cup dry red wine**
- 2 **15- to 19-ounce cans
  cannellini (white kidney)
  beans, rinsed and
  drained**
- 2 **14-ounce cans chicken
  broth**
- 1 **28-ounce can crushed
  tomatoes**
- 1 **teaspoon salt**
- ¼ **teaspoon crushed red
  pepper**
- 10 **ounces ditali pasta
  (1½ cups)**
- ¼ **cup snipped fresh basil**
- 1 **tablespoon snipped fresh
  oregano**
  **Fresh oregano leaves
  (optional)**

1 In a 4-quart Dutch oven, cook onion, pancetta, and garlic in hot oil over medium heat for about 5 minutes or until onion is tender, stirring occasionally. Add wine, scraping up any crusty browned bits.

2 Stir in drained beans, broth, tomatoes, salt, and crushed red pepper. Bring to boiling; reduce heat. Simmer, covered, for 20 minutes.

3 Meanwhile, cook pasta according to package directions; drain. Stir cooked pasta, basil, and snipped oregano into bean mixture. If desired, garnish with oregano leaves.

Nutrition facts per serving: 415 cal., 9 g total fat (2 g sat. fat), 11 mg chol., 1577 mg sodium, 68 g carb., 19 g protein.

cioppino

Prep: 45 minutes
Cook: 30 minutes
Makes: 4 servings

- 8 fresh clams in shells
- 2 8-ounce fresh or frozen lobster tails
- 8 ounces fresh or frozen fish fillets (such as halibut, red snapper, perch, or sea bass)
- 8 ounces fresh or frozen peeled and deveined shrimp
- ½ cup sliced fresh mushrooms
- ⅓ cup chopped green or red sweet pepper
- ¼ cup chopped onion
- 2 cloves garlic, minced
- 1 tablespoon olive oil
- 1 14.5-ounce can diced tomatoes, undrained
- ⅓ cup dry red wine or white wine
- ¼ cup water
- 2 tablespoons snipped fresh parsley
- 2 tablespoons tomato paste
- 1 tablespoon lemon juice
- 1½ teaspoons snipped fresh basil, or ½ teaspoon dried basil, crushed
- 1½ teaspoons snipped fresh oregano, or ½ teaspoon dried oregano, crushed
- 1 teaspoon sugar
- ¼ teaspoon salt
- ⅛ teaspoon crushed red pepper

1 Using a stiff brush, scrub clam shells under cold running water. In a large pot or bowl, combine 8 cups water and 3 tablespoons salt. Add clams; soak for 15 minutes. Drain and rinse clams; discard water. Repeat soaking, draining, and rinsing two more times.

2 Meanwhile, thaw lobster, fish, and shrimp, if frozen. Remove and discard skin from fish, if present. Rinse lobster, fish, and shrimp; pat dry with paper towels. Cut fish into 1½-inch pieces. Cover and chill lobster, fish, and shrimp until needed.

3 In a 4- to 5-quart Dutch oven, cook mushrooms, sweet pepper, onion, and garlic in hot oil until tender. Stir in tomatoes, wine, the ¼ cup water, the parsley, tomato paste, lemon juice, dried basil and oregano (if using), sugar, the ¼ teaspoon salt, and the crushed red pepper. Bring to boiling; reduce heat. Cover and simmer for 20 minutes.

4 Add lobster and fresh basil and oregano (if using). Return to boiling; reduce heat. Cover and simmer for 5 minutes. Add clams, fish, and shrimp. Return to boiling; reduce heat. Cover and simmer for 5 to 10 minutes more or until clams open, fish flakes easily, and lobster and shrimp are opaque. Discard any unopened clams.

Nutrition facts per serving: 326 cal., 6 g total fat (1 g sat. fat), 255 mg chol., 1181 mg sodium, 13 g carb., 50 g protein.

italian DUTCH OVEN CHOWDER

To enjoy this hearty chowder as the Italians do, be sure to include the oysters.

Start to Finish: 55 minutes
Makes: 8 to 10 side-dish
servings

4   slices bacon

2   large carrots, sliced ½ inch thick

2   medium parsnips, sliced ½ inch thick; cut larger pieces in half

2   medium onions, cut into thin wedges

3   medium potatoes, chopped

2   14-ounce cans reduced-sodium chicken broth

½   teaspoon garlic salt

¼   teaspoon ground black pepper

3   tablespoons margarine or butter, melted

3   tablespoons all-purpose flour

2   cups milk

2   cups frozen whole kernel corn

1   pint shucked oysters with liquid (optional)

    Snipped fresh chives or parsley (optional)

1 In a 4-quart Dutch oven, cook bacon until crisp. Remove bacon, reserving 1 tablespoon drippings in the pan. Drain bacon on paper towels; crumble and set aside.

2 Add carrots, parsnips, and onions to Dutch oven. Cook over medium heat for 8 to 10 minutes or until brown, stirring occasionally.

3 Add potatoes, chicken broth, garlic salt, and pepper. Bring to boiling; reduce heat. Cover and simmer for about 15 minutes or until potatoes are tender. (At this point the soup can be cooled, covered, and chilled in the refrigerator overnight.)

4 In a small mixing bowl, stir together melted margarine or butter and flour. Stir flour-margarine mixture, milk, and corn into chowder mixture in Dutch oven.

5 Cook and stir over medium heat until slightly thickened. If desired, add oysters and liquid to soup; heat through. Sprinkle each serving with crumbled bacon and chives or parsley, if desired.

Nutrition facts per serving: 267 cal., 13 g total fat (6 g sat. fat), 23 mg chol., 566 mg sodium, 33 g carb., 7 g protein.

italian SPINACH SOUP

Each bowl of this brothy soup holds a healthful portion of greens. In the produce aisle, look for peppery watercress with small dark green leaves. If unavailable, use arugula.

Start to Finish: 35 minutes
Makes: 6 side-dish servings

1 **medium onion, chopped**

4 **cloves garlic, minced**

2 **teaspoons dried Italian seasoning, crushed**

2 **tablespoons butter**

2 **tablespoons dry sherry (optional)**

2 **14-ounce cans chicken broth**

1 **large potato, peeled and chopped**

2 **9-ounce packages fresh spinach, or 1¼ pounds fresh spinach, washed and trimmed**

Salt

2 **cups watercress, tough stems removed**

2 **ounces Parmesan cheese, shaved**

2 **small tomatoes, quartered, seeded, and thinly sliced**

1 In 4-quart Dutch oven, cook onion, garlic, and Italian seasoning in hot butter over medium heat for 5 minutes or until onion is tender, stirring occasionally.

2 If using sherry, remove Dutch oven from heat; slowly pour in sherry. Return to heat; cook and stir for 1 minute. Add broth and potato. Bring to boiling. Simmer, covered, for 10 minutes or until potato is tender. Remove from heat.

3 Set aside 2 cups of the spinach. Stir remaining spinach, half at a time, into soup just until wilted. Cook for about 5 minutes.

4 Transfer soup, half at a time, to food processor or blender; cover and process or blend until smooth. Return to Dutch oven; heat through. Season with salt.

5 To serve, top with reserved spinach, watercress, Parmesan, and tomatoes.

Nutrition facts per serving: 151 cal., 7 g total fat (4 g sat. fat), 18 mg chol., 881 mg sodium, 16 g carb., 8 g protein.

roasted TOMATO-VEGETABLE SOUP

Prep: 35 minutes
Cook: 25 minutes
Makes: 6 servings

- 1 **tablespoon olive oil**
- ½ **cup chopped onion**
- ½ **cup chopped celery**
- ½ **cup chopped carrot**
- 2 **cloves garlic, minced**
- 3 **14-ounce cans reduced-sodium chicken broth**
- 2 **cups peeled, seeded, and coarsely chopped butternut squash**
- 1 **14.5-ounce can fire-roasted diced tomatoes, undrained**
- 1 **15- to 19-ounce can cannellini beans (white kidney beans), rinsed and drained**
- 1 **small zucchini, halved lengthwise and sliced**
- 1 **cup broccoli and/or cauliflower florets**
- 1 **tablespoon snipped fresh oregano, or 1 teaspoon dried oregano, crushed**
- ¼ **teaspoon salt**
- ¼ **teaspoon ground black pepper**
  Freshly shredded Parmesan cheese (optional)

① In a 4-quart Dutch, oven heat oil over medium heat. Add onion, celery, carrot, and garlic; cook and stir for 5 minutes.

② Stir in chicken broth, squash, and tomatoes. Bring to boiling; reduce heat. Cover and simmer for 20 minutes. Add cannellini beans, zucchini, broccoli, oregano, salt, and pepper; cook for 5 minutes more. If desired, sprinkle individual servings with Parmesan cheese.

Nutrition facts per serving: 131 cal., 3 g total fat (0 g sat. fat), 0 mg chol., 855 mg sodium, 24 g carb., 9 g protein.

Slow Cooker Directions: Omit olive oil. In a 3½- or 4-quart slow cooker, combine onion, celery, carrot, garlic, chicken broth, squash, tomatoes, cannellini beans, and dried oregano (if using). Cover and cook on low-heat setting for 7 to 8 hours or on high-heat setting for 3½ to 4 hours. If using low-heat setting, turn to high-heat setting. Add zucchini, broccoli, fresh oregano (if using), salt, and pepper. Cover and cook for 30 minutes more. Serve as above.

minestrone

Convenience products galore, such as chicken broth preseasoned with favorite Italian flavors, and canned tomatoes cut down on the need for measuring out a long list of ingredients.

Start to Finish: 30 minutes
Makes: 4 servings

2 **14-ounce cans seasoned chicken broth with Italian herbs**

2 **medium carrots, thinly sliced (1 cup)**

½ **cup ditalini or tiny bow-tie pasta**

1 **medium zucchini, chopped (1¼ cups)**

1 **14.5-ounce can diced tomatoes with onions and garlic, undrained**

1 **15- to 15.5-ounce can white kidney beans (cannellini) or navy beans, rinsed and drained**

¼ **cup slivered fresh basil or spinach**

Bottled hot pepper sauce (optional)

1 Combine broth and carrots in a large saucepan. Bring to boiling; reduce heat. Simmer, covered, for 5 minutes.

2 Stir in pasta and simmer, uncovered, for 8 minutes or until pasta is just tender. Add zucchini, tomatoes, and beans; heat through. Sprinkle each serving with basil or spinach just before serving. If desired, pass bottled hot pepper sauce at the table.

Nutrition facts per serving: 203 cal., 2 g total fat (0 g sat. fat), 0 mg chol., 1328 mg sodium, 38 g carb., 14 g protein.

salads

Gremolata Shrimp Salad, *page 78*

italian WEDDING SALAD

Reminiscent of the famous Italian wedding soup, this warm pasta salad combines hearty meatballs, spinach, and orzo pasta.

Start to Finish: 25 minutes
Makes: 4 main-dish
servings

6   ounces orzo

1   16-ounce package frozen
    cooked meatballs (32),
    thawed

½   cup bottled Italian
    dressing

1   6-ounce jar marinated
    artichoke hearts, drained
    and chopped

1   6-ounce package baby
    spinach

¼   cup chopped walnuts,
    toasted

    Salt and ground black
    pepper

    Finely shredded
    Parmesan or Romano
    cheese (optional)

1 Cook pasta according to package directions. Drain well.

2 In a 4-quart Dutch oven, combine meatballs and salad dressing; cook over medium heat until meatballs are heated through, stirring occasionally. Stir in drained pasta, artichoke hearts, spinach, and walnuts. Heat and stir just until spinach is wilted. Season to taste with salt and pepper. If desired, sprinkle with Parmesan cheese.

Nutrition facts per serving: 730 cal., 52 g total fat (15 g sat. fat), 40 mg chol., 1383 mg sodium, 48 g carb., 23 g protein.

grilled CHICKEN PASTA SALAD

Prep: 20 minutes
Cook: 10 minutes
Grill: 4 minutes
Makes: 8 servings

- 1 **pound rotini**
- 2 **pounds thin-sliced chicken cutlets**
- 2 **tablespoons lemon juice**
- 1 **large red sweet pepper, cored, seeded, and diced**
- 1 **large green sweet pepper, cored, seeded, and diced**
- 1 **medium red onion, halved and thinly sliced**
- 2 **scallions, trimmed and thinly sliced**
- 2 **tablespoons minced fresh dill**
- 1 **cup light mayonnaise**
- ½ **cup red wine vinegar**
- ½ **cup honey**
- 1 **teaspoon mustard**
- 1 **teaspoon sugar**
- 1 **teaspoon onion powder**
- 1 **teaspoon dried parsley**
- ¼ **teaspoon salt**
- ¼ **teaspoon ground black pepper**
- ½ **cup canola oil**

1 Cook pasta according to package directions.

2 While pasta is cooking, heat grill pan or broiler. Sprinkle chicken with the lemon juice and grill or broil for about 2 minutes per side or until internal temperature reads 160°F on an instant-read thermometer. Let cool.

3 Cut chicken into bite-size pieces and mix with cooled pasta in a large bowl. Add diced peppers, onion, scallions, and dill.

4 In a medium bowl, whisk mayonnaise, vinegar, honey, mustard, sugar, onion powder, parsley flakes, salt, and black pepper. Gradually whisk in oil.

5 Pour mayonnaise mixture over pasta and chicken and toss. Refrigerate until ready to serve.

Nutrition facts per serving: 514 cal., 25 g total fat (3 g sat. fat), 76 mg chol., 409 mg sodium, 43 g carb., 30 g protein.

warm chicken SALAD
WITH PEPPERS AND PINE NUTS

Prep: 25 minutes
Bake: 14 minutes
Oven: 400°F
Makes: 8 servings

10 ounces ciabatta or crusty country bread, crust removed and torn or cut into 1-inch pieces

1 clove garlic, minced

¼ cup olive oil

1 2- to 2½-pound purchased roasted chicken, warm

1 medium red sweet pepper, cut into thin strips

1 medium yellow sweet pepper, cut into thin strips

½ cup Kalamata olives, pitted and halved

¼ cup pine nuts

2 tablespoons olive oil

8 ounces arugula or packaged mixed salad greens

½ cup fresh basil leaves, shredded

¼ cup balsamic vinegar

¼ cup olive oil

Salt and ground black pepper

1 Preheat oven to 400°F. In a medium bowl, combine bread pieces and garlic. Drizzle with ¼ cup oil; toss gently to coat. Transfer bread pieces to a 15x10x1-inch baking pan. Spread in a single layer. Bake for 6 to 8 minutes or until bread pieces are golden brown.

2 Meanwhile, remove and discard skin from chicken. Pull meat from bones; discard bones. Cut meat into bite-size pieces and place in a very large serving bowl. Add toasted bread pieces to chicken.

3 In the same baking pan, combine sweet peppers, olives, and pine nuts. Drizzle with the 2 tablespoons oil; toss gently to coat. Spread in a single layer. Bake for 8 to 10 minutes or until sweet peppers are tender and nuts are toasted. Add pepper mixture to chicken mixture.

4 Add half of the arugula and half of the basil to chicken mixture; toss gently to combine. Repeat with the remaining arugula and the remaining basil.

5 For dressing: In a small bowl, whisk together balsamic vinegar and ¼ cup oil. Pour dressing over chicken mixture; toss gently to coat. Season to taste with salt and pepper. Serve immediately.

Nutrition facts per serving: 446 cal., 31 g total fat (6 g sat. fat), 63 mg chol., 792 mg sodium, 25 g carb., 19 g protein.

arugula AND PEAR SALAD

Peppery arugula teams up with creamy Gorgonzola and sweet pears for a beautiful start to a stylish dinner party.

Start to Finish: 25 minutes
Makes: 6 side-dish servings

- ¼ **cup olive oil**
- 2 **tablespoons balsamic vinegar**
- ¼ **teaspoon salt**
- 2 **ounces pancetta, or 3 slices bacon, cut into bite-size pieces**
- 2 **medium firm, ripe pears (such as Anjou or Bosc), cored and thinly sliced**
- 1 **5-ounce package arugula (about 7 cups)**
- 6 **very thin slices red onion, separated into rings**
- ¼ **cup pine nuts, toasted**
- 1 **ounce Gorgonzola cheese, crumbled**

  Ground black pepper (optional)

1. For dressing, in a screw-top jar, combine olive oil, balsamic vinegar, and salt. Cover and shake well. Set aside.

2. In a large skillet, cook pancetta or bacon over medium heat until crisp. Remove from skillet; drain on paper towels. Set aside. Add pear slices to drippings in skillet; cook for 5 to 7 minutes or until lightly browned and tender, stirring occasionally. Keep warm.

3. In a very large bowl, combine arugula, onion slices, and dressing. Toss gently to coat with dressing.

4. Divide arugula mixture among six salad plates. Arrange pears on top. Sprinkle with pancetta, pine nuts, and Gorgonzola cheese. If desired, sprinkle with pepper.

Nutrition facts per serving: 215 cal., 17 g total fat (4 g sat. fat), 11 mg chol., 343 mg sodium, 12 g carb., 4 g protein.

pizza SALAD

Premade pizza crusts and packaged salad greens, Canadian bacon, and shredded cheese make this recipe child's play — just open packages and toss.

Start to Finish: 20 minutes
Makes: 4 main-dish servings

- ¾ **cup bottled fat-free Western or French salad dressing**
- 1 **tablespoon snipped fresh basil or oregano**
- 1 **10-ounce package (8 cups) torn romaine lettuce**
- 1 **8-ounce package (two 6-inch) Italian bread shells, torn into bite-size pieces**
- 1 **cup chopped Canadian-style bacon or pepperoni**
- 1 **cup shredded reduced-fat mozzarella cheese or pizza cheese (4 ounces)**

1 For dressing, in a small bowl, combine the Western or French salad dressing and the basil or oregano.

2 In an extra-large bowl, toss together lettuce, bread shell pieces, Canadian-style bacon or pepperoni, and cheese. Transfer to dinner plates. Drizzle each serving with dressing. Toss salad lightly to coat.

Nutrition facts per serving: 363 cal., 11 g total fat (4 g sat. fat), 39 mg chol., 1357 mg sodium, 40 g carb., 24 g protein.

Test Kitchen Tip: If you don't have fresh herbs on hand, use ½ teaspoon dried basil or oregano instead.

antipasto SALAD

You'll find all the wonderful flavors of Italian antipasto in this vegetable-packed side dish.

Prep: 20 minutes
Chill: 4 hours
Makes: 10 to 12 side-dish servings

2 **medium tomatoes, cut into bite-size pieces (1⅓ cups)**

1 **small zucchini, sliced (1 cup)**

1 **small yellow summer squash, sliced (1 cup)**

1 **cup cauliflower florets**

1 **cup broccoli florets**

1 **small cucumber, sliced (1 cup)**

2 **stalks celery, sliced (1 cup)**

1 **medium green sweet pepper, cut into bite-size pieces (¾ cup)**

1 **medium carrot, sliced (½ cup)**

½ **of a small red onion, sliced and separated into rings**

½ **cup pitted black olives or pimiento-stuffed green olives**

½ **cup pepperoncini salad peppers**

1 **cup bottled Italian dressing**

1 **8-ounce package sliced salami, cut into bite-size pieces**

1 In a very large bowl,* combine all of the ingredients, tossing to coat mixture with dressing.

2 Cover and chill in the refrigerator for at least 4 hours or up to 24 hours, tossing occasionally.

Nutrition facts per serving: 186 cal., 15 g total fat (4 g sat. fat), 21 mg chol., 987 mg sodium, 8 g carb., 7 g protein.

*Note: If you combine and seal all the ingredients in a large, heavy plastic bag, simply turn the bag occasionally instead of tossing the ingredients.

creamy LEMON-DILL TUNA SALAD

Start to Finish: 20 minutes
Makes: 6 servings

Creamy Lemon-Dill Dressing*

- 1 15- to 19-ounce can cannellini beans (white kidney beans), rinsed and drained
- 1 12-ounce can solid white tuna (water-pack), drained and broken into chunks
- ½ cup halved red onion slices
- ½ cup bottled roasted yellow or red sweet peppers, drained and chopped
- 1 stalk celery, sliced
- 2 to 3 tablespoons capers, drained, or ½ cup stuffed green olives,** sliced (optional)
- ½ 5-ounce package arugula or baby spinach
- 2 large tomatoes, sliced

Prepare dressing. In bowl, combine beans, tuna, and half the dressing. Stir in onions, peppers, celery, and capers. Serve over greens and tomato slices. Pass remaining dressing at the table.

***Creamy Lemon-Dill Dressing:** In a small bowl, combine ¾ cup mayonnaise or salad dressing, 1 tablespoon Dijon-style mustard, 1 tablespoon lemon juice, 1 tablespoon snipped fresh dill, 1 tablespoon honey, ¼ teaspoon salt, and ⅛ teaspoon ground black pepper. Makes about 1 cup.

Nutrition facts per serving: 343 cal., 23 g total fat (3 g sat. fat), 35 mg chol., 686 mg sodium, 18 g carb., 20 g protein.

****Tip:** Look beyond pimiento-stuffed olives for olives stuffed with almonds, jalapeños, onions, garlic, or other fun treats!

marinated SEAFOOD SALAD

Prep: 30 minutes
Chill: 2 to 4 hours
Stand: 15 minutes
Makes: 8 servings

12 ounces fresh or frozen peeled and deveined medium shrimp (with tails intact)

8 ounces fresh or frozen bay scallops

8 ounces fresh or frozen cleaned squid

2 tablespoons olive oil

½ cup pitted Kalamata olives

½ cup pitted green olives

⅓ cup olive oil

3 tablespoons lemon juice

2 tablespoons finely chopped shallot

2 tablespoons snipped fresh oregano

1 tablespoon snipped fresh chives

2 cloves garlic, minced

¼ teaspoon salt

⅛ to ¼ teaspoon crushed red pepper

1 large bunch watercress or 4 cups fresh baby spinach

Freshly cracked black pepper

1 Thaw shrimp, scallops, and squid, if frozen. If desired, remove tails from shrimp. Rinse shrimp and scallops; pat dry with paper towels. Rinse squid; drain in a colander. Cut squid into thin strips. Set aside.

2 In a large skillet, heat the 2 tablespoons oil over medium heat. Add shrimp; cook and stir for 2 to 3 minutes or until shrimp are opaque. Using a slotted spoon, transfer shrimp to a large bowl.

3 Add scallops to hot skillet; cook and stir for 1 to 2 minutes or until scallops are opaque. Using a slotted spoon, transfer scallops to the bowl.

4 Add squid to hot skillet; cook and stir for 1 to 2 minutes or until squid is opaque. Using a slotted spoon, transfer squid to the bowl. Stir in olives.

5 For dressing: In a screw-top jar, combine the ⅓ cup oil, lemon juice, shallot, oregano, chives, garlic, salt, and crushed red pepper. Cover and shake well. Pour dressing over seafood mixture; toss gently to coat. Cover and chill for 2 to 4 hours.

6 To serve, let seafood mixture stand at room temperature for 15 minutes. Divide watercress among eight salad plates. Using a slotted spoon, spoon seafood mixture on top of watercress. Sprinkle with cracked black pepper.

Nutrition facts per serving: 237 cal., 16 g total fat (2 g sat. fat), 140 mg chol., 418 mg sodium, 5 g carb., 18 g protein.

gremolata SHRIMP SALAD

A simple garnish of parsley, garlic, and lemon zest, gremolata typically offsets rich meat dishes, although here it perks up grilled shrimp.

Start to Finish: 40 minutes
Makes: 4 servings

- 1 **pound fresh or frozen medium shrimp in shells**
- **Salt and ground black pepper**
- 6 **cups arugula and/or fresh spinach leaves**
- 1½ **cups cherry tomatoes, halved**
- 1 **cup crumbled ricotta salata cheese (4 ounces)**
- ¼ **cup snipped fresh Italian (flat-leaf) parsley**
- 2 **teaspoons finely shredded lemon peel**
- 2 **cloves garlic, minced**
- ½ **teaspoon cracked black pepper**
- ¼ **cup olive oil**
- 2 **tablespoons lemon juice**
- 2 **tablespoons white wine vinegar**

1 Thaw shrimp, if frozen. Peel and devein shrimp, leaving tails intact, if desired. Rinse shrimp; pat dry with paper towels. Thread shrimp onto skewers.* Sprinkle with salt and ground pepper.

2 Heat a greased grill pan on the stove over medium heat. Place shrimp skewers in grill pan. Cook for 6 to 8 minutes or until shrimp are opaque, turning once.

3 In a large bowl, combine arugula, tomatoes, and ricotta salata. Divide shrimp skewers and arugula mixture among dinner plates.

4 For gremolata, in a small bowl, combine parsley, lemon peel, garlic, and cracked pepper. For dressing, in a screw-top jar, combine half of the gremolata, the oil, lemon juice, and vinegar. Cover and shake well. Season to taste with additional salt. Drizzle dressing over salads; sprinkle with the remaining gremolata.

Nutrition facts per serving: 347 cal., 22 g total fat (2 g sat. fat), 197 mg chol., 808 mg sodium, 6 g carb., 30 g protein.

Broiling Directions: Preheat broiler. Place shrimp skewers on the unheated rack of a broiling pan. Broil 4 to 5 inches from the heat for 6 to 8 minutes or until shrimp are opaque, turning once.

***Note:** Be sure skewers are no longer than your grill pan so that they will lay flat in the pan. Shrimp may be cooked in the grill pan without skewers, but skewers make it easier to turn the shrimp.

eggplant PARMESAN STACKS WITH GREENS

Prep: 30 minutes
Bake: 2 hours
Oven: 400°F
Makes: 4 servings

1 small head garlic

Eggplant:

½ **cup seasoned bread crumbs**

½ **teaspoon salt**

¼ **teaspoon black pepper**

¼ **teaspoon ground nutmeg**

2 **egg whites**

1 **eggplant (about 1½ pounds),
  cut into 12 ½-inch-thick slices**

½ **cup shredded part-skim
  mozzarella cheese
  (2 ounces)**

¼ **cup grated Parmesan cheese**

Sauce:

8 **ounces grape tomatoes,
  halved**

½ **cup basil leaves, sliced**

1 **teaspoon dried oregano**

¼ **teaspoon salt**

⅛ **teaspoon black pepper**

Dressing and Salad:

  Roasted garlic

¼ **cup balsamic vinegar**

⅛ **teaspoon salt**

⅛ **teaspoon black pepper**

⅛ **teaspoon dried oregano**

¼ **cup extra virgin olive oil**

8 **cups mixed greens**

1 Preheat oven to 400°F. Peel papery skin from head of garlic. Cut ½-inch slice from top pointed end of garlic. Coat cut end of bulb with nonstick cooking spray. Wrap in foil and roast in 400°F oven for about 1 hour or until cloves are soft and golden brown. Set aside.

2 For eggplant, on a sheet of waxed paper, mix together bread crumbs, salt, pepper, and nutmeg. In pie plate or large shallow dish, lightly whisk the egg whites with 1 tablespoon water.

3 Coat large baking sheet with nonstick cooking spray. Dip each slice of eggplant into egg whites and then into the bread crumb mixture, coating both sides. Place eggplant slices on prepared baking sheet.

4 Bake for 45 minutes, until nicely browned and tender.

5 For sauce, in a small bowl, combine the grape tomatoes, sliced basil, oregano, salt, and pepper.

6 Overlap the eggplant slices slightly on the baking sheet into 4 stacks, 3 slices per stack. Spoon the sauce over each stack; evenly sprinkle mozzarella and Parmesan cheeses over the tomatoes. Bake for an additional 10 minutes.

7 For dressing and salad, while eggplant is baking, squeeze roasted garlic cloves out of the whole head and into bowl; gently mash cloves against side of bowl with fork. Whisk in balsamic vinegar, salt, pepper, and oregano until fairly smooth. Gradually drizzle in olive oil, while whisking continuously.

8 Toss greens with dressing. Serve 2 cups dressed salad with each eggplant stack.

Nutrition facts per serving: 320 cal., 19 g total fat (5 g sat. fat), 13 mg chol., 1210 mg sodium, 27 g carb., 13 g protein.

italian RICE SALAD

Prep: 30 minutes
Chill: 1 hour
Makes: 6 servings

Garlic Vinaigrette*

3   cups cooked, slightly
    warm basmati or long
    grain white rice**

1   cup chopped red, green,
    and/or orange sweet
    pepper

1   6-ounce jar quartered
    marinated artichoke
    hearts, drained

⅓   cup chopped red onion

¼   cup raisins

2   tablespoons drained
    capers

    Mixed salad greens,
    mesclun, or torn
    romaine

    Fresh basil leaves
    (optional)

1 Prepare the Garlic Vinaigrette.

2 In a large bowl, combine rice, sweet pepper, artichokes, red onion, raisins, and capers. Stir vinaigrette and drizzle over rice mixture; toss gently to coat. Cover and chill for at least 1 hour or up to 24 hours. Serve rice salad on a bed of salad greens. If you like, garnish with basil.

*Garlic Vinaigrette: In a small bowl, whisk together ½ cup canola oil or safflower oil; ⅓ cup snipped fresh Italian (flat-leaf) parsley; ¼ cup white wine vinegar; 3 tablespoons snipped fresh dill or 2 teaspoons dried dillweed; 1 teaspoon sea salt; 1 teaspoon freshly ground black pepper; 1 teaspoon snipped fresh basil or ¼ teaspoon dried basil, crushed; 1 teaspoon snipped fresh oregano or ¼ teaspoon dried oregano, crushed; and 2 cloves garlic, minced. Use immediately or cover and store in the refrigerator for up to 3 days. Makes about ¾ cup.

Nutrition facts per serving: 325 cal., 20 g total fat (1 g sat. fat), 0 mg chol., 447 mg sodium, 33 g carb., 4 g protein.

Tip: To cook rice, place 1 cup uncooked basmati or long grain white rice in a fine-mesh sieve. Run cool water over the rice for several minutes; drain well. In a medium saucepan, bring 2 cups water to boiling. Slowly add rice and return to boiling; reduce heat. Simmer, covered, for 15 to 20 minutes or until liquid is absorbed and rice is tender. Remove from heat and let cool for about 15 minutes. Makes 3 cups.

panzanella

Generations of Italians have put day-old bread to good use with this inspired bread salad.
Use end-of-season heirloom tomatoes in a variety of hues for a stunning effect.

Prep: 20 minutes
Bake: 6 minutes
Stand: 15 minutes
Oven: 450°F
Makes: 4 servings

3 **cups Italian bread cubes**

2 **tablespoons olive oil**

1½ **cups coarsely chopped tomatoes (3 medium)**

½ **of a small red onion, cut into thin wedges and separated**

¼ **cup snipped fresh basil or Italian (flat-leaf) parsley**

2 **tablespoons red or white wine vinegar**

2 **tablespoons olive oil**

2 **cloves garlic, minced**

¼ **teaspoon salt**

¼ **teaspoon ground black pepper**

4 **cups torn or chopped romaine lettuce**

1 Preheat oven to 450°F. Place bread cubes in a shallow baking pan. Drizzle with 2 tablespoons oil; toss gently to coat. Bake for about 6 minutes or until toasted, stirring once or twice. Let cool.

2 In a large bowl, combine bread cubes, tomatoes, onion, and basil.

3 For dressing, in a screw-top jar, combine vinegar, oil, garlic, salt, and pepper. Cover and shake well. Pour dressing over bread mixture; toss gently to coat.

4 Let stand for 15 minutes to allow the flavors to blend. Serve bread mixture over lettuce.

Nutrition facts per serving: 268 cal., 15 g total fat (2 g sat. fat), 0 mg chol., 416 mg sodium, 28 g carb., 5 g protein.

Note: To save time, substitute ¼ to ⅓ cup bottled Italian dressing for the homemade dressing.

roasted BEET AND PARSLEY SALAD

Prep: 25 minutes
Chill: 2 to 24 hours
Roast: 1 hour 15 minutes
Oven: 350°F
Makes: 6 servings

- 4 **medium fresh beets with tops**
- 2 **tablespoons water**
- 3 **medium carrots, cut into thin bite-size strips**
- 1 **large orange, peeled and sectioned**
- 2 **tablespoons olive oil**
- 2 **tablespoons balsamic vinegar**
- 1 **teaspoon sugar**
- ½ **teaspoon salt**
- ¼ **teaspoon ground black pepper**
- 1 **tablespoon olive oil**
- ½ **cup fresh flat-leaf parsley leaves**
- ⅓ **cup pine nuts, toasted**

1 Preheat oven to 350°F. Scrub beets; trim off stem and root ends, reserving tops. Do not peel beets. Remove stems from beet tops; measure 2 cups greens and set aside. Place beets on a foil-lined baking sheet; sprinkle with the water. Bring up two opposite edges of foil; seal with a double fold. Fold remaining ends to completely enclose beets, leaving space for steam to build. Roast for about 1¼ hours or until beets are tender. Let cool until easy to handle. Slip off skins; transfer beets to a medium bowl. Cover and chill for 2 to 24 hours.

2 Cut beets into wedges; return to the bowl. Add carrots and orange.

3 For dressing, in a small screw-top jar, combine the 2 tablespoons oil, the balsamic vinegar, sugar, salt, and pepper. Cover and shake well. Pour over beet mixture; toss gently to coat.

4 In a large skillet, heat the 1 tablespoon oil over medium-high heat. Add the reserved 2 cups beet greens; cook and stir for about 1 minute or just until wilted.

5 Transfer wilted beet greens to a serving platter. Using a slotted spoon, transfer beet mixture to platter, reserving dressing. Sprinkle salad with parsley and pine nuts. Serve with the reserved dressing.

Nutrition facts per serving: 162 cal., 11 g total fat (2 g sat. fat), 0 mg chol., 261 mg sodium, 14 g carb., 4 g protein.

insalata MISTA

Insalata mista means "mixed salad" in Italian. Create a mixture of your own using the best selections from your grocery store. Or if you're short on time, buy mesclun, a blend of young, small salad greens.

Start to Finish: 25 minutes
Makes: 4 servings

- 2 tablespoons olive oil or salad oil
- 2 tablespoons balsamic vinegar
- 2 teaspoons snipped fresh oregano or basil
- ⅛ teaspoon salt
- ⅛ teaspoon ground black pepper
- 4 cups torn mixed salad greens (such as radicchio, spinach, arugula, and/or chicory)
- 1 cup yellow and/or red cherry tomatoes, halved
- ¼ cup snipped fresh oregano or basil
- ½ cup pitted black olives
- 3 ounces thinly sliced fresh mozzarella cheese

1 For dressing, in a screw-top jar, combine oil, balsamic vinegar, the 2 teaspoons oregano, the salt, and pepper. Cover and shake well to combine.

2 In a large serving bowl, toss together salad greens, cherry tomatoes, the ¼ cup oregano, and the olives. Shake dressing again and drizzle over salad; toss to coat. Top with mozzarella cheese.

Nutrition facts per serving: 166 cal., 13 g total fat (4 g sat. fat), 15 mg chol., 298 mg sodium, 7 g carb., 5 g protein.

ricotta AND VEGETABLES

Start to Finish: 30 minutes
Makes: 6 to 8 servings

4   cups broccoli florets or
    cut-up broccolini

2½ cups fresh asparagus or
    green beans cut into
    1-inch pieces

1   15-ounce carton ricotta
    cheese

½   cup snipped fresh basil

¼   cup grated Parmesan or
    Romano cheese

2   tablespoons balsamic
    vinegar

2   tablespoons olive oil

1   tablespoon snipped fresh
    thyme, or 1 teaspoon
    dried thyme, crushed

1   teaspoon salt

1   teaspoon ground black
    pepper

2   cloves garlic, minced

3   large ripe tomatoes,
    seeded and chopped

12 to 16 ounces dried
    tubular pasta, cooked
    and drained

1 In a Dutch oven, cook broccoli and asparagus in a large amount of boiling water for 3 minutes; drain.

2 In a large bowl, combine broccoli and asparagus, ricotta cheese, basil, Parmesan cheese, vinegar, oil, thyme, salt, pepper, and garlic. Gently stir in tomatoes.

3 Add broccoli mixture to hot cooked pasta; toss gently to combine.

Nutrition facts per serving: 443 cal., 16 g total fat (7 g sat. fat), 39 mg chol., 529 mg sodium, 56 g carb., 21 g protein.

romano BEAN SALAD

Prep: 25 minutes
Stand: 30 minutes
Makes: 4 to 6 servings

¼ cup finely chopped shallot

2 cloves garlic, minced

1 tablespoon olive oil

1 16-ounce package frozen cut Italian green beans, thawed

2 tablespoons fresh marjoram leaves

½ teaspoon salt

⅛ teaspoon ground black pepper

½ cup cherry tomatoes, halved

1 tablespoon balsamic vinegar

1 In a large skillet, cook shallots and garlic in hot oil over medium heat for 2 minutes. Add Italian beans, marjoram, salt, and pepper. Cook for 8 to 10 minutes or just until beans are tender, stirring occasionally. Remove from heat.

2 Stir in tomatoes and balsamic vinegar. Cool for at least 30 minutes; serve within 2 hours. Stir gently before serving.

Nutrition facts per serving: 78 cal., 4 g total fat (1 g sat. fat), 0 mg chol., 305 mg sodium, 11 g carb., 2 g protein.

caprese-style TOMATOES

Start to Finish: 25 minutes
Makes: 4 servings

4 small tomatoes (3 to
 4 ounces each)

3 tablespoons olive oil

3 tablespoons white wine
 vinegar

½ teaspoon sugar

16 to 24 fresh basil leaves

3 ounces fresh mozzarella
 or buffalo mozzarella
 cheese, drained and cut
 into 8 slices

¼ cup chopped red onion

 Sea salt or salt

 Freshly ground black
 pepper

1 Using a serrated knife, cut a thin slice off the bottom of each tomato so it will stand upright. Cut each tomato crosswise into three slices; set aside.

2 For vinaigrette, in a screw-top jar, combine oil, vinegar, and sugar. Cover and shake well.

3 To assemble, place 2 or 3 basil leaves on the bottom slice of each tomato. Top each with a slice of cheese and some of the onion. Repeat layering tomato slices, basil, cheese, and onion. Add the top slice of each tomato. Serve with vinaigrette, salt, and pepper.

Nutrition facts per serving: 178 cal., 15 g total fat (4 g sat. fat), 17 mg chol., 189 mg sodium, 5 g carb., 6 g protein.

knife-and-fork
CAESAR SALAD

Attention anchovy lovers—tired of picking through a Caesar salad to get a taste of your favorite ingredient? This salad brings the anchovies front and center.

Prep: 30 minutes
Bake: 20 minutes
Oven: 300°F
Makes: 6 side-dish
  servings

Caesar Dressing*

Parmesan Croutons**

3 hearts of romaine lettuce, quartered lengthwise

6 canned anchovy fillets, halved lengthwise

1 ounce Parmesan cheese, shaved (optional)

Chill six salad plates. Prepare Caesar Dressing and Parmesan Croutons. To serve, place 2 romaine wedges on each chilled plate. Drizzle with Caesar Dressing. Top each salad with 2 anchovy strips, Parmesan Croutons, and, if desired, shaved Parmesan cheese.

*Caesar Dressing: In a blender or food processor, combine 3 cloves garlic, 3 canned anchovy fillets, and 2 tablespoons fresh lemon juice. Cover and blend or process until mixture is smooth, scraping sides of container as necessary. Add ¼ cup olive oil, 1 hard-cooked egg yolk, 1 teaspoon Dijon-style mustard, and ½ teaspoon sugar. Blend or process until smooth. Use immediately or cover and chill for up to 24 hours. Stir before using.

**Parmesan Croutons: Preheat oven to 300°F. Cut four ½-inch-thick slices Italian or French bread into 1-inch cubes (you should have about 3½ cups). In a large skillet, melt ¼ cup butter. Remove from heat. Stir in 3 tablespoons grated Parmesan cheese and 2 finely minced garlic cloves. Add bread cubes, stirring until cubes are coated with butter mixture. Spread bread cubes in a single layer in a shallow baking pan. Bake for 10 minutes; stir. Bake for about 10 minutes more or until bread cubes are crisp and golden. Cool completely; store in an airtight container for up to 24 hours.

Nutrition facts per serving: 262 cal., 21 g total fat (8 g sat. fat), 65 mg chol., 521 mg sodium, 13 g carb., 8 g protein.

florentine PASTA SALAD

Refrigerated pesto sauce becomes a handy dressing for this yummy linguine salad.

Start to Finish: 25 minutes
Makes: 4 side-dish
      servings

- **2 ounces linguine or fettuccine**
- **½ cup purchased refrigerated pesto sauce**
- **1 tablespoon lemon juice**
- **1 cup shredded fresh spinach**
- **½ cup seeded tomato, coarsely chopped**
- **1 small red onion, thinly sliced (⅓ cup)**
- **2 tablespoons pine nuts or slivered almonds, toasted**

1 Cook pasta according to package directions. Drain pasta; rinse with cold water. Drain again.

2 In a large mixing bowl, combine pesto sauce and lemon juice. Add pasta; toss to coat.

3 Add spinach, tomato, and red onion to pasta mixture; toss until mixed. Sprinkle with nuts. Serve immediately.

Nutrition facts per serving: 224 cal., 15 g total fat (0 g sat. fat), 2 mg chol., 150 mg sodium, 19 g carb., 6 g protein.

pizza, SANDWICHES, AND BREADS

Grilled Florentine Flank Steak Sandwiches, *page 112*

meat LOVER'S DEEP DISH

Prep: 10 minutes
Cook: 5 minutes
Bake: 30 minutes
Oven: 450°F
Makes: 8 servings

1 **tablespoon olive oil**

8 **ounces ground beef**

8 **ounces sweet or hot Italian pork sausage**

½ **teaspoon dried Italian seasoning**

1 **pound pizza dough, at room temperature, or 1 batch Basic Pizza Dough***

2 **cups shredded mozzarella cheese**

½ **green sweet pepper, seeded and thinly sliced**

1 **cup marinara sauce**

2 **tablespoons grated Parmesan cheese**

1 Preheat oven to 450°F. Lightly coat a 10-inch deep-dish pizza pan with olive oil.

2 Heat oil in a large nonstick skillet over medium-high heat. Crumble in the ground beef and sausage; season with the Italian seasoning and cook for 4 to 5 minutes or until meat is no longer pink. Set aside.

3 On a lightly floured surface, roll out the dough to form a circle slightly larger than the pan. Place dough in prepared pan, pressing excess dough to the sides.

4 Layer 1½ cups mozzarella cheese, reserved meat mixture, pepper, and sauce onto dough. Bake for 15 minutes. Top with the remaining ½ cup mozzarella and Parmesan cheese. Bake for an additional 15 minutes. Remove from oven and allow to cool slightly.

5 Use a sharp knife to cut into 8 slices, then remove with pie server or spatula.

*Basic Pizza Dough: Place 1 cup warm water (about 110°F) in a small bowl and stir in 1 package (.25 ounce) active dry yeast. In a large bowl, whisk together 2½ cups of flour, 1 teaspoon sugar, and 1 teaspoon salt. Make a well in the center and add the yeast mixture and 2 tablespoons olive oil. Stir until dough comes together and forms a ball. Turn out onto a well-floured surface and knead for 5 minutes, adding ¼ cup flour (or as much as needed). Form into a disk and place in a bowl that has been lightly coated with olive oil. Turn disk over and cover bowl with plastic wrap. Allow to rise in a warm place for 2 hours. Remove dough from bowl and punch down. Roll out to desired diameter.

Nutrition facts per serving: 350 cal., 19 g total fat (7 g sat. fat), 49 mg chol., 768 mg sodium, 29 g carb., 19 g protein.

steak AND CHEESE MELT PIZZA

Prep: 10 minutes
Cook: 10 minutes
Broil: 5 minutes
Makes: 6 servings

- 1 **tablespoon vegetable oil**
- 2 **large onions, thinly sliced (about 1 pound)**
- 1¼ **teaspoons steak seasoning**
- 2 **8-ounce boneless strip steaks, cut ½ to ¾ inch thick**
- 1 **12-inch Italian bread shell**
- 2 **tablespoons deli-style mustard**
- 1 **cup shredded mild cheddar cheese (4 ounces)**
- 1 **cup shredded provolone cheese (4 ounces)**

1 Preheat broiler. In a large skillet, heat oil over medium heat. Add onions and ½ teaspoon of the steak seasoning. Cook for about 10 minutes or onion is lightly browned, stirring occasionally,

2 Meanwhile, coat the rack of an unheated broiler pan with cooking spray. Sprinkle steaks with the remaining ¾ teaspoon steak seasoning; place on prepared broiler pan. Broil 3 to 4 inches from heat for about 4 minutes or until desired doneness, turning once halfway through broiling. Transfer steaks to cutting board; thinly slice across the grain.

3 Place bread shell on the broiler pan; spread with mustard. Sprinkle half of the cheddar cheese and half of the provolone cheese over the top. Top with steak and cooked onion. Sprinkle the remaining cheddar and provolone cheese over steak and onion. Broil for about 1 minute or until cheese is melted and steak is heated. Transfer pizza to a cutting board; cut into 6 wedges.

Nutrition facts per serving: 490 cal., 23 g total fat (10 g sat. fat), 79 mg chol., 849 mg sodium, 35 g carb., 34 g protein.

meatball-filled
DOUBLE-CRUST PIZZA

Prep: 10 minutes
Bake: 20 minutes
Cool: 5 minutes
Oven: 450°F
Makes: 8 servings

- 2 **pounds frozen pizza dough, thawed**
- ⅔ **cup pizza sauce**
- 1 **teaspoon dried oregano**
- 2 **cups shredded Italian cheese blend**
- 1 **12-ounce package fully cooked Italian-style turkey meatballs, cut into ¼-inch-thick slices**
- 1 **cup ricotta cheese**
- ½ **cup sliced turkey pepperoni (2 ounces)**

1 Place oven rack in lowest position. Preheat oven to 450°F. Coat 12-inch pizza pan with nonstick cooking spray.

2 On well-floured surface with a floured rolling pin, roll out half of the pizza dough into 12-inch round, rolling from the center of the dough to the edge and turning the dough frequently to keep dough even. Carefully lift the dough into prepared pizza pan, gently fitting it in pan.

3 Spoon the pizza sauce evenly over dough, leaving a ½-inch border all around the edge. Sprinkle evenly with oregano, then 1 cup of the cheese blend, up to the ½-inch border. Scatter the sliced meatballs over cheese. Sprinkle the remaining 1 cup cheese blend over the top. Spoon on the ricotta cheese, dolloping evenly up to the border. Arrange the sliced pepperoni over the ricotta.

4 Roll out the other pound of pizza dough as in step 1 into a 12-inch round. Gently lift and fit over the filling on the pizza. Line up the edge with the bottom crust, gently pulling if necessary. Crimp the top edge with lower edge as you would with a pie. Cut slits in the top for steam vents.

5 Bake the pizza on the bottom rack in the oven for 20 to 25 minutes or until the crust is nicely browned and the filling is heated through. Let the pizza cool for 5 to 10 minutes before slicing into 8 wedges.

Nutrition facts per serving: 534 cal., 17 g total fat (8 g sat. fat), 72 mg chol., 1033 mg sodium, 63 g carb., 29 g protein.

white PIZZA WITH SMOKED TURKEY

Prep: 10 minutes
Bake: 10 minutes
Oven: 450°F
Makes: 12 servings

2 **large thin-crust Italian pizza bread shells (two 10-ounce packages)**

2 **cups shredded Italian blend cheese**

4 **ounces thinly sliced smoked turkey, cut into ½-inch-wide strips**

1 **15-ounce container ricotta cheese**

1 **4-ounce container garlic-and-herb cheese spread**

¼ **cup thinly sliced fresh basil**

1 Preheat oven to 450°F.

2 Place each crust on a baking sheet. Sprinkle 1 cup shredded cheese over each pizza shell. Evenly distribute turkey over each.

3 In small bowl, mix ricotta and cheese spread. Evenly dollop over each pizza.

4 Bake until heated through and cheese is melted, about 10 minutes. Sprinkle the basil over the pizzas. To serve, cut each into 6 equal wedges.

Nutrition facts per serving: 302 cal., 15 g total fat (8 g sat. fat), 48 mg chol., 583 mg sodium, 25 g carb., 15 g protein.

sicilian-style
PEPPERONI PIZZA

Prep: 10 minutes
Bake: 20 minutes
Oven: 500°F
Makes: 12 servings

- **2 pounds pizza dough, at room temperature, or 1 batch Basic Pizza Dough***
- **1 cup marinara sauce**
- **½ teaspoon dried oregano**
- **2 cups shredded mozzarella cheese**
- **2 ounces sliced pepperoni (about ⅓ cup)**

1 Preheat oven to 500°F. Coat a 15x10x1-inch baking pan with nonstick cooking spray.

2 On a lightly floured surface, roll dough into a 15x10-inch rectangle. Gently roll up onto a lightly floured rolling pin and unroll onto prepared pan. Push dough into corners.

3 Spread sauce evenly over dough to within ½ inch of edge. Sprinkle oregano over sauce. Scatter cheese over top. Place pepperoni slices over cheese. Bake for 18 to 20 minutes or until nicely browned on bottom. Remove from oven.

4 Cool slightly and cut into 12 slices; serve.

*Basic Pizza Dough: Place 1 cup warm water (about 110°F) in a small bowl and stir in 1 package (.25 ounce) active dry yeast. In a large bowl, whisk together 2½ cups of flour, 1 teaspoon sugar, and 1 teaspoon salt. Make a well in the center and add the yeast mixture and 2 tablespoons olive oil. Stir until dough comes together and forms a ball. Turn out onto a well-floured surface and knead for 5 minutes, adding ¼ cup flour (or as much as needed). Form into a disk and place in a bowl that has been lightly coated with olive oil. Turn disk over and cover bowl with plastic wrap. Allow to rise in a warm place for 2 hours. Remove dough from bowl and punch down. Roll out to desired diameter.

Nutrition facts per serving: 255 cal., 10 g total fat (4 g sat. fat), 21 mg chol., 582 mg sodium, 35 g carb., 10 g protein.

cherry TOMATO AND PROSCIUTTO FOCACCIA

Prep: 15 minutes
Bake: 14 minutes
plus 15 minutes
Roast: 30 minutes
Oven: 425°F, 325°F
Makes: 8 servings

1 **pound frozen pizza dough, thawed**

2 **tablespoons grated Parmesan cheese**

1½ **pounds cherry tomatoes, halved**

1 **large shallot, minced**

2 **garlic cloves, minced**

1 **tablespoon balsamic vinegar**

½ **teaspoon salt**

¼ **teaspoon ground black pepper**

2 **cups baby arugula**

8 **ounces mozzarella cheese, shredded (2 cups)**

3 **ounces thinly sliced prosciutto, cut or torn lengthwise into ½-inch strips**

2 **tablespoons fresh basil, sliced into ribbons**

1 Preheat oven to 425°F. Roll and stretch dough into a large rimmed baking sheet, at least 15x10x1 inches. Sprinkle with Parmesan cheese and bake for 14 minutes or until lightly browned. Remove from oven and set aside. Reduce oven temperature to 325°F.

2 Toss together tomatoes, shallot, garlic, vinegar, salt, and pepper in a medium bowl. Spread tomatoes in an even layer in a rimmed baking sheet and roast for 30 minutes. Remove from oven and gently stir in arugula.

3 Sprinkle 1 cup of the mozzarella over dough and scatter tomato mixture over top using a slotted spoon. Distribute prosciutto slices over tomatoes. Sprinkle remaining mozzarella over top and bake at 325°F for 15 minutes. Cool on wire rack for 5 minutes, then sprinkle with basil and cut into 8 pieces.

Nutrition facts per serving: 293 cal., 10 g total fat (5 g sat. fat), 28 mg chol., 772 mg sodium, 35 g carb., 15 g protein.

smoky VEGETABLE PIZZA

Prep: 15 minutes
Cook: 4 minutes
Bake: 20 minutes
Oven: 500°F
Makes: 8 servings

2 tablespoons olive oil

3 cloves garlic, chopped

½ bunch broccoli raab, cut into 1-inch pieces

½ red sweet pepper, seeded and sliced

½ red onion, thinly sliced

4 ounces cremini mushrooms, sliced

¼ teaspoon salt

¼ teaspoon ground black pepper

1 pound pizza dough, at room temperature, or 1 batch Basic Pizza Dough*

1 cup marinara sauce

8 ounces smoked mozzarella cheese, shredded (2 cups)

1 Preheat oven to 500°F. Coat a 14-inch pizza pan with nonstick cooking spray.

2 Heat olive oil in a large nonstick skillet over medium-high heat. Stir in garlic, broccoli raab, red pepper, onion, mushrooms, salt, and pepper. Cook for 4 minutes, stirring occasionally.

3 On a lightly floured surface, roll out dough into a 14-inch circle. Gently roll up onto a lightly floured rolling pin and unroll onto prepared pizza pan.

4 Spread sauce over dough to within ½ inch of edge. Sprinkle 1½ cups of cheese over sauce. Evenly spoon the vegetables over cheese. Scatter the remaining cheese over vegetables. Bake for 18 to 20 minutes or until nicely browned on bottom.

5 Cool slightly and cut into 8 slices; serve.

*Basic Pizza Dough: Place 1 cup warm water (about 110°F) in a small bowl and stir in 1 package (.25 ounce) active dry yeast. In a large bowl, whisk together 2½ cups of flour, 1 teaspoon sugar, and 1 teaspoon salt. Make a well in the center and add the yeast mixture and 2 tablespoons olive oil. Stir until dough comes together and forms a ball. Turn out onto a well-floured surface and knead for 5 minutes, adding ¼ cup flour (or as much as needed). Form into a disk and place in a bowl that has been lightly coated with olive oil. Turn disk over and cover bowl with plastic wrap. Allow to rise in a warm place for 2 hours. Remove dough from bowl and punch down. Roll out to desired diameter.

Nutrition facts per serving: 275 cal., 13 g total fat (4 g sat. fat), 22 mg chol., 644 mg sodium, 31 g carb., 12 g protein.

cheesy RED PEPPER PIZZA

Prep: 15 minutes
Bake: 15 minutes
Oven: 425°F
Makes: 8 servings

1   **13.8-ounce package refrigerated pizza dough**

1   **tablespoon olive oil**

½   **cup sliced roasted red and/or yellow sweet peppers**

2   **medium roma tomatoes, thinly sliced**

2   **tablespoons shredded fresh spinach (optional)**

1   **cup shredded mozzarella cheese (4 ounces)**

¼   **teaspoon coarsely ground black pepper**

2   **tablespoons snipped fresh basil**

1 Preheat oven to 425°F. Coat a 12-inch pizza pan with nonstick spray. Press refrigerated dough into prepared pan, building up edges. Brush with olive oil. Bake for 10 minutes.

2 Remove crust from oven. Arrange sweet pepper, tomato slices, and, if using, spinach on the crust. Sprinkle with cheese and black pepper.

3 Bake for 5 to 10 minutes more or until cheese is bubbly. Sprinkle with basil and cut into 8 wedges.

Nutrition facts per serving: 182 cal., 6 g total fat (2 g sat. fat), 9 mg chol., 359 mg sodium, 25 g carb., 8 g protein.

classic MARGHERITA PIZZA

Prep: 10 minutes
Bake: 13 minutes
Oven: 500°F
Makes: 8 servings

1 **pound pizza dough, at room temperature, or 1 batch Basic Pizza Dough***

¾ **cup marinara sauce**

¼ **teaspoon dried oregano**

6 **ounces fresh mozzarella cheese, thinly sliced**

1 **tablespoon grated Parmesan cheese**

8 **fresh basil leaves**

1 Preheat oven to 500°F. Coat a 14-inch pizza pan with nonstick cooking spray.

2 On a lightly floured surface, roll out dough into a 14-inch circle. Gently roll up onto a lightly floured rolling pin and unroll onto prepared pizza pan.

3 Spread sauce evenly over dough to within ½ inch of edge. Sprinkle oregano over the sauce. Arrange mozzarella over the top and sprinkle with Parmesan. Bake for 12 to 13 minutes or until nicely browned on bottom. Remove from oven.

4 Garnish with basil. Cool slightly and cut into 8 slices; serve.

***Basic Pizza Dough:** Place 1 cup warm water (about 110°F) in a small bowl and stir in 1 package (.25 ounce) active dry yeast. In a large bowl, whisk together 2½ cups of flour, 1 teaspoon sugar, and 1 teaspoon salt. Make a well in the center and add the yeast mixture and 2 tablespoons olive oil. Stir until dough comes together and forms a ball. Turn out onto a well-floured surface and knead for 5 minutes, adding ¼ cup flour (or as much as needed). Form into a disk and place in a bowl that has been lightly coated with olive oil. Turn disk over and cover bowl with plastic wrap. Allow to rise in a warm place for 2 hours. Remove dough from bowl and punch down. Roll out to desired diameter.

Nutrition facts per serving: 207 cal., 9 g total fat (4 g sat. fat), 16 mg chol., 495 mg sodium, 27 g carb., 9 g protein.

four CHEESE WHITE PIZZA

Prep: 10 minutes
Cook: 2½ minutes
Bake: 15 minutes
Oven: 500°F
Makes: 8 servings

2 **tablespoons olive oil**

4 **cloves garlic, coarsely chopped**

1 **6-ounce bag baby spinach**

1 **pound pizza dough, at room temperature, or 1 batch Basic Pizza Dough***

1 **cup shredded mozzarella cheese (4 ounces)**

½ **cup shredded provolone cheese (2 ounces)**

½ **cup shredded Asiago cheese (2 ounces)**

¾ **cup ricotta cheese**

2 **tablespoons toasted pine nuts**

1 Preheat oven to 500°F. Coat a 14-inch pizza pan with nonstick cooking spray.

2 Heat 1 tablespoon of the oil in a medium nonstick skillet over medium-high heat. Add garlic and cook for 30 seconds. Gradually add spinach and cook until wilted, about 2 minutes. Remove from heat.

3 On a lightly floured surface, roll out dough into a 14-inch circle. Gently roll up onto a lightly floured rolling pin and unroll onto prepared pizza pan.

4 In a medium bowl, mix together mozzarella, provolone, and Asiago cheeses. Sprinkle half of the cheese mixture over the dough. Evenly spoon the spinach over the cheese. Drizzle any oil and garlic from the skillet over the spinach. Sprinkle the remaining cheese mixture over the spinach. Dollop tablespoons of the ricotta cheese over top. Drizzle remaining 1 tablespoon olive oil over the pizza. Bake for 14 to 15 minutes or until nicely browned on bottom.

5 To serve, scatter pine nuts over the top and cut into 8 slices.

***Basic Pizza Dough:** Place 1 cup warm water (about 110°F) in a small bowl and stir in 1 package (.25 ounce) active dry yeast. In a large bowl, whisk together 2½ cups of flour, 1 teaspoon sugar, and 1 teaspoon salt. Make a well in the center and add the yeast mixture and 2 tablespoons olive oil. Stir until dough comes together and forms a ball. Turn out onto a well-floured surface and knead for 5 minutes, adding ¼ cup flour (or as much as needed). Form into a disk and place in a bowl that has been lightly coated with olive oil. Turn disk over and cover bowl with plastic wrap. Allow to rise in a warm place for 2 hours. Remove dough from bowl and punch down. Roll out to desired diameter.

Nutrition facts per serving: 308 cal., 17 g total fat (7 g sat. fat), 32 mg chol., 449 mg sodium, 29 g carb., 14 g protein.

grilled FLORENTINE FLANK STEAK SANDWICHES

Prep: 30 minutes
Marinate: 8 to 24 hours
Grill: 17 to 21 minutes
Makes: 6 sandwiches

- 1 **1-pound beef flank steak**
- 2 **tablespoons balsamic vinegar**
- 2 **tablespoons olive oil**
- 2 **tablespoons lemon juice**
- 2 **teaspoons Dijon-style mustard**
- 1 **teaspoon fennel seeds, crushed**
- 2 **cloves garlic, minced**
- 1 **15-ounce can Great Northern beans, rinsed and drained**
- ¼ **cup sour cream**
- 2 **tablespoons finely shredded Parmesan cheese**
- 1 **tablespoon finely chopped onion**
- 1 **tablespoon snipped fresh parsley**
- 1 **tablespoon capers, drained**
- ½ **teaspoon lemon-pepper seasoning**
- 1 **medium onion, cut into ½-inch-thick slices**
- 6 **4- to 6-inch ciabatta or other Italian rolls, split and toasted**
- 1 **cup fresh baby spinach**
- ½ **cup bottled roasted red sweet peppers, drained and cut into strips**

1 Trim fat from steak. Score both sides of steak in a diamond pattern, making shallow diagonal cuts at 1-inch intervals. Place steak in a large resealable plastic bag set in a shallow dish. In a small bowl, whisk together balsamic vinegar, oil, lemon juice, mustard, fennel seeds, and garlic. Reserve 2 tablespoons of the marinade. Pour the remaining marinade over steak. Seal bag; turn to coat steak. Marinate in the refrigerator for 8 to 24 hours, turning bag occasionally.

2 In a medium bowl, mash beans with a potato masher. Stir in the reserved 2 tablespoons marinade, the sour cream, Parmesan cheese, chopped onion, parsley, capers, and lemon-pepper seasoning. Set spread aside.

3 Drain steak, discarding marinade. Place steak and onion slices on the rack of an uncovered grill directly over medium coals. Grill steak for 17 to 21 minutes for medium doneness (160°F), turning once halfway through grilling. Add onion slices to grill rack during the last 5 minutes; grill until tender and slightly charred, turning once.

4 To serve, thinly slice steak diagonally across the grain. Spread cut sides of ciabatta rolls with bean spread. Fill the rolls with spinach, steak slices, roasted peppers, and grilled onion slices.

Nutrition facts per sandwich: 439 cal., 12 g total fat (4 g sat. fat), 30 mg chol., 840 mg sodium, 56 g carb., 29 g protein.

italian BEEF SANDWICHES

The meat for these sandwiches is cooked in a slow cooker. Let it simmer all day long for an evening gathering.

Prep: 25 minutes
Cook: 10 to 11 hours (low) or 5 to 5½ hours (high)
Makes: 10 to 12 sandwiches

- 1 4-pound boneless beef sirloin or beef rump roast, cut into 2- to 3-inch pieces
- ½ cup water
- 1 0.7-ounce envelope Italian dry salad dressing mix
- 2 teaspoons dried Italian seasoning, crushed
- ½ to 1 teaspoon crushed red pepper
- ½ teaspoon garlic powder
- 10 to 12 hoagie buns, kaiser rolls, or other sandwich rolls, split
- 1½ cups shredded Italian blend cheese (6 ounces; optional)

  Pickles, sliced onion, sliced pepperoncini, and/or roasted red sweet pepper strips (optional)

1 Place beef in a 4- or 5-quart slow cooker. In a small bowl, combine water, salad dressing mix, Italian seasoning, crushed red pepper, and garlic powder; pour over beef in slow cooker. Cover and cook on low-heat setting for 10 to 11 hours or on high-heat setting for 5 to 5½ hours.

2 Remove meat from cooker with a slotted spoon. Using two forks, shred the meat. Serve meat in rolls. If you like, sprinkle sandwiches with cheese and place sandwiches on two large baking sheets; broil sandwiches, one pan at a time, 4 to 5 inches from the heat for 1 to 2 minutes or until cheese is melted.

3 Strain cooking juices through a fine-mesh sieve. Drizzle each sandwich with some of the strained juices to moisten. If you like, top each sandwich with pickles, onion, pepperoncini, and/or roasted red sweet pepper strips. Serve remaining cooking juices for dipping, if you like.

Nutrition facts per sandwich: 564 cal., 19 g total fat (7 g sat. fat), 117 mg chol., 921 mg sodium, 51 g carb., 44 g protein.

italian-style BURGERS

Try these sophisticated basil-scented burgers at your next picnic or cookout. They're sure to be a big hit!

Prep: 15 minutes
Chill: 1 hour
Grill: 14 to 18 minutes
Makes: 8 burgers

½ **cup fine dry bread crumbs**

½ **cup finely chopped onion**

⅓ **cup milk**

2 **tablespoons grated Parmesan cheese**

1 **tablespoon dried basil, crushed**

½ **teaspoon garlic salt**

¼ **teaspoon ground black pepper**

1½ **pounds lean ground beef**

8 **slices provolone cheese**

8 **kaiser rolls with sesame seeds, split and toasted**

Lettuce (optional)

Yellow and/or red tomato slices (optional)

Marinara sauce, warmed (optional)

❶ In a medium bowl, stir together bread crumbs, onion, milk, Parmesan cheese, basil, garlic salt, and pepper. Add meat; mix well. Shape meat mixture into eight ¾-inch-thick patties. Place patties in a shallow container. Cover and chill for 1 hour.

❷ Place patties on the rack of an uncovered grill directly over medium coals. Grill for 14 to 18 minutes or until done (160°F),* turning once halfway through grilling and topping each burger with a cheese slice for the last 1 minute of grilling.

❸ Serve burgers on rolls. If desired, top with lettuce, tomatoes, and/or a spoonful of pasta sauce.

Nutrition facts per burger: 464 cal., 22 g total fat (10 g sat. fat), 74 mg chol., 823 mg sodium, 36 g carb., 29 g protein.

*Note: The internal color of a burger is not a reliable doneness indicator. A beef patty cooked to 160°F is safe, regardless of color. To measure the doneness of a patty, insert an instant-read thermometer through the side of the patty to a depth of 2 to 3 inches.

chicken-olive CALZONES

Whether served warm with spaghetti sauce or at room temperature from a lunch bag, these pizza-flavored turnovers will be a family favorite.

Prep: 25 minutes
Bake: 10 minutes
Stand: 5 minutes
Oven: 425°F
Makes: 6 calzones

1½ **cups chopped cooked chicken (8 ounces)**

½ **cup shredded Monterey Jack cheese (2 ounces)**

¼ **cup chopped celery**

¼ **cup chopped pitted black olives**

½ **teaspoon dried basil, crushed**

¼ **teaspoon dried oregano, crushed**

⅛ **teaspoon garlic powder**

⅛ **teaspoon ground black pepper**

⅓ **cup tub-style cream cheese with chives and onion**

1 **13.8-ounce package refrigerated pizza dough**

1 **egg, lightly beaten**

1 **tablespoon water**

Grated Parmesan cheese (optional)

Spaghetti sauce, warmed (optional)

1 Preheat oven to 425°F. For filling, in a medium bowl, combine chicken, Monterey Jack cheese, celery, olives, basil, oregano, garlic powder, and pepper. Stir in cream cheese.

2 For calzones, unroll pizza dough. On lightly floured surface, roll dough into a 15x10-inch rectangle. Cut into six 5-inch squares. Divide chicken-olive filling among the squares. Brush edges with water. Lift one corner and stretch dough over to the opposite corner. Seal edges of dough well with tines of a fork. Arrange calzones on a greased baking sheet. Prick tops with a fork. In a small bowl, combine egg and 1 tablespoon water; brush over the calzones. If desired, sprinkle with Parmesan cheese.

3 Bake for 10 to 12 minutes or until golden. Let stand for 5 minutes before serving. If desired, serve with warm spaghetti sauce.

Nutrition facts per calzone: 268 cal., 13 g total fat (5 g sat. fat), 90 mg chol., 320 mg sodium, 19 g carb., 18 g protein.

italian TURKEY SANDWICHES

Basil-flecked mayonnaise and roasted sweet peppers take these sandwiches from ordinary to extraordinary.

Start to Finish: 20 minutes
Makes: 4 sandwiches

⅓ cup fine dry bread crumbs

2 teaspoons dried Italian seasoning, crushed

2 turkey tenderloins (about 1 pound total)

2 teaspoons olive oil

2 tablespoons snipped fresh basil, or ½ teaspoon dried basil, crushed

¼ cup light mayonnaise dressing or salad dressing

8 ½-inch slices Italian bread, toasted

1 cup bottled roasted red and/or yellow sweet peppers, cut into thin strips

1 In a large plastic bag, combine bread crumbs and Italian seasoning. Slice each turkey tenderloin in half horizontally to make ½-inch-thick steaks. Place steaks in the bag one at a time; seal and shake to coat.

2 In a 12-inch nonstick skillet, heat oil over medium heat. Add turkey steaks; cook for about 10 minutes or until no longer pink (170°F); turn once halfway through cooking time.

3 In a small bowl, stir 1 tablespoon of the snipped basil (if using) or the ½ teaspoon dried basil into the mayonnaise dressing. Spread dressing mixture on one side of 4 bread slices. Top bread slices with turkey steaks, sweet pepper strips, and the remaining snipped basil (if using). Top with remaining bread slices and serve.

Nutrition facts per sandwich: 399 cal., 11 g total fat (2 g sat. fat), 73 mg chol., 671 mg sodium, 40 g carb., 33 g protein.

italian HERO CALZONES

Save the oil drained from the dried tomatoes to brush on the dough before baking.
The coating of oil helps the calzones bake to an even golden brown.

Prep: 20 minutes
Bake: 15 minutes
Oven: 425°F
Makes: 4 calzones

- **2 tablespoons cornmeal**
- **⅓ cup snipped oil-packed dried tomatoes**
- **1 cup chopped cooked meat (such as smoked turkey, smoked sausage, cooked chicken, ham, and/or pepperoni)**
- **⅓ cup chopped pitted ripe olives**
- **1½ cups shredded mozzarella cheese (6 ounces)**
- **1 13.8-ounce package refrigerated pizza dough**
- **Finely shredded or grated Parmesan cheese**
- **Cayenne pepper (optional)**
- **Purchased pizza or pasta sauce, warmed**

1 Preheat to oven 425°F. Lightly grease a large baking sheet and sprinkle with cornmeal; set aside. Well drain dried tomatoes, reserving oil; set aside. In a medium bowl combine cooked meat, olives, and tomatoes. Stir in mozzarella cheese.

2 Unroll pizza dough. On a lightly floured surface, roll or stretch pizza dough to a 14-inch square. Cut dough into four 7-inch squares. Divide meat mixture among squares, positioning it on one half of each square. Brush dough edges with water. Fold dough over filling to form rectangles or triangles, stretching dough as needed. Seal edges by pressing with the tines of a fork.

3 Place calzones on prepared baking sheet. Brush tops with reserved oil; sprinkle with Parmesan cheese and, if desired, cayenne pepper. Bake about 15 minutes or until golden brown. Serve warm with warmed pizza sauce.

Nutrition Facts per calzone: 423 cal., 17 g total fat (7 g sat. fat), 54 mg chol., 1095 mg sodium, 44 g carb., 23 g protein.

quick STROMBOLI

Prep: 20 minutes
Bake: 25 minutes
Oven: 375°F
Makes: 8 servings

1 **1-pound loaf frozen whole wheat or white bread dough, thawed**

8 **ounces lean cooked ham, thinly sliced**

⅓ **cup shredded mozzarella cheese (1½ ounces)**

¼ **cup pitted black olives, coarsely chopped**

¼ **cup pimiento-stuffed green olives, coarsely chopped**

⅛ **teaspoon crushed red pepper**

1 **tablespoon reduced-fat milk**

1 **tablespoon finely shredded Parmesan cheese (optional)**

1 Preheat oven to 375°F. Line a 15x10x1-inch baking pan with foil; grease foil. Set pan aside.

2 On a lightly floured surface, roll bread dough into a 15x8-inch rectangle. (If dough is difficult to roll out, cover and let rest for a few minutes.) Arrange ham on top of dough rectangle to within ½ inch of the edges. Top with mozzarella cheese, olives, and crushed red pepper. Brush edges with a little water.

3 Starting from a long side, roll up into a spiral; pinch edge to seal. Pinch ends and tuck under spiral. Place, seam side down, in the prepared baking pan. Brush with milk. Using a sharp knife, make shallow diagonal cuts at 2-inch intervals along the top to allow steam to escape. If desired, sprinkle with Parmesan cheese.

4 Bake for 25 to 30 minutes or until brown. If necessary, cover loosely with foil after 20 minutes of baking to prevent overbrowning.

Nutrition facts per serving: 201 cal., 5 g total fat (1 g sat. fat), 15 mg chol., 746 mg sodium, 28 g carb., 13 g protein.

antipasto ITALIAN PANINI

This hearty sandwich, like a grinder gone to finishing school, is not only authentic but also amazing. Slice it into quarters for picnics and tailgating or slender wedges for party portions.

Prep: 20 minutes
Grill: 12 minutes
Makes: 4 servings

- 1 9- to 10-inch Italian flatbread (focaccia)
- 2 tablespoons butter, softened
- ¼ cup olive tapenade and/or pesto
- 4 ounces sliced provolone cheese
- 3 ounces sliced salami
- 3 ounces sliced capicola
- 4 pepperoncini
- 6 large fresh basil leaves

1 Cut focaccia in half horizontally. If necessary, trim off the tops or bottoms of the focaccia halves to make each about ¾ inch thick. Spread the outsides with butter. Spread the insides with tapenade.

2 With the tapenade side up, arrange half of the provolone cheese on one of the focaccia halves. Add salami, capicola, pepperoncini, and basil. Top with the remaining provolone cheese and the remaining focaccia half, tapenade side down.

3 For a charcoal grill, arrange medium-hot coals around the outside edge of grill. Test for medium heat in center of grill. Place sandwich on grill rack in center of grill. Place a baking sheet on top of the sandwich and weight it down with two bricks. Cover and grill for 6 to 8 minutes or until bread is golden brown and cheese is melted. Turn sandwich and weight down. Cover and grill for 6 to 8 minutes more or until bread is golden brown and cheese is melted. (For a gas grill, preheat grill. Reduce heat to medium. Adjust for indirect cooking. Grill as above.) To serve, cut into 4 wedges.

Nutrition facts per serving: 604 cal., 35 g total fat (13 g sat. fat), 78 mg chol., 1912 mg sodium, 51 g carb., 25 g protein.

italian PIZZA SANDWICHES

Some like it hot! If you do, choose the hot sausage. For those with less adventurous palates, choose the mild or sweet sausage. You may want to grill some of each.

Prep: 15 minutes
Grill: 20 minutes
Makes: 4 sandwiches

1 **medium green sweet pepper, cut into thin strips**

1 **medium onion, thinly sliced**

1 **tablespoon margarine or butter**

4 **fresh mild or hot Italian sausage links (¾ to 1 pound)**

½ **cup pizza sauce**

4 **individual French-style rolls, split**

2 **tablespoons grated Parmesan cheese**

1 Tear off a 36x18-inch piece of heavy foil. Fold in half to make a double thickness of foil that measures 18x18 inches. Place sweet pepper and onion in the center of the foil. Dot with margarine or butter. Bring up two opposite edges of foil and seal with double fold. Then fold remaining ends to completely enclose, leaving space for steam to build. Prick the sausage links in several places with a fork or the tip of a sharp knife.

2 Arrange preheated coals around a drip pan in a covered grill. Test for medium heat above the pan. Place sausage links and the foil packet on grill over drip pan. Cover and grill for 20 to 25 minutes or until sausage juices run clear and vegetables are tender.

3 Meanwhile, heat pizza sauce in a small saucepan. Toast cut sides of buns on grill.

4 To serve, halve sausage links lengthwise, cutting to but not through the other side. Place sausage links in the toasted rolls. Top each with pepper mixture and pizza sauce. Sprinkle with Parmesan cheese.

Nutrition facts per sandwich: 376 cal., 22 g total fat (7 g sat. fat), 51 mg chol., 1067 mg sodium, 26 g carb., 18 g protein.

taleggio-pear PANINI

When warmed, Taleggio—Italy's luscious washed-rind cheese—wraps around thinly sliced pears like a velvety soft blanket.

Prep: 20 minutes
Freeze: 1 to 2 hours
Grill: 7 minutes per batch
Makes: 4 sandwiches

8 ounces **Taleggio or Brie cheese, rind removed if necessary**

8 **slices crusty country whole grain or Italian bread**

¼ **cup butter, softened**

1¼ **cups thinly sliced Bosc and/or Anjou pear**

3 **tablespoons honey**

1 If using Taleggio cheese, place it in the freezer for 1 to 2 hours or until partially frozen; cut cheese into ¼-inch slices. If using Brie cheese, cut rounds in half horizontally, then in half vertically. Set aside.

2 Preheat an electric sandwich press, a covered indoor grill, a grill pan, or a 12-inch skillet. Spread both sides of bread slices with butter. Place bread slices, a few at a time, in the sandwich press or indoor grill. Cover and cook for about 6 minutes or until bread is lightly toasted. (If using a grill pan or skillet, place bread slices in pan. Weight bread down with a heavy skillet or a pie plate containing a can of vegetables. Cook until bread is lightly toasted. Turn bread over, weight down, and cook until bread is lighty toasted.)

3 Immediately layer cheese and pear slices on half of the bread slices; drizzle with honey. Top with the remaining bread slices. Cook for about 1 minute or just until cheese is melted.

Nutrition facts per sandwich: 509 cal., 28 g total fat (8 g sat. fat), 31 mg chol., 433 mg sodium, 51 g carb., 16 g protein.

panini WITH GRILLED MUSHROOMS

Prep: 15 minutes
Grill: 10 minutes
Makes: 4 sandwiches

- 3 6- to 8-ounce portobello mushrooms
- 3 tablespoons garlic-flavored oil or olive oil
- 3 tablespoons red wine vinegar
- 6 cloves garlic, minced
- ½ teaspoon ground black pepper
- ¼ teaspoon salt
- 4 small crusty rolls, split and toasted
- Garlic-flavored oil or olive oil (optional)
- 2 medium tomatoes, sliced ¼ inch thick
- 4 ounces sliced mozzarella cheese
- 2 cups arugula or fresh baby spinach

1 Cut off mushroom stems even with caps; discard stems. Lightly rinse mushroom caps; gently pat dry with paper towels. Using a knife or a teaspoon, gently scrape away the gills (the black portions underneath the caps).

2 In a small bowl, whisk together 3 tablespoons oil, vinegar, garlic, pepper, and salt. Brush both sides of mushroom caps with oil mixture.

3 For a charcoal grill, grill mushroom caps, top sides down, on the rack of an uncovered grill directly over medium coals for 5 minutes. Turn and grill for 5 to 7 minutes more or until slightly softened and tender, brushing with the remaining oil mixture. (For a gas grill, preheat grill. Reduce heat to medium. Place mushroom caps on grill rack over heat. Cover and grill as above.) Cut mushrooms into ½-inch slices.

4 If desired, brush cut sides of toasted rolls with additional oil. Place tomato slices on bottoms of rolls. Layer with mushroom slices, cheese, and arugula. Replace tops of rolls. If necessary, secure with wooden skewers.

Nutrition facts per sandwich: 392 cal., 18 g total fat (5 g sat. fat), 14 mg chol., 659 mg sodium, 42 g carb., 17 g protein.

portobello BURGERS

Start to Finish: 20 minutes
Makes: 4 burgers

4   **portobello mushrooms**

2   **tablespoons olive oil**

1   **teaspoon dried Italian seasoning, crushed**

4   **slices provolone cheese**

4   **ciabatta rolls, split**

¼   **cup mayonnaise**

4   **to 8 pieces bottled, roasted red sweet pepper**

¾   **cup fresh basil leaves**

1 Scrape gills from mushroom caps, if desired. Drizzle mushrooms with oil. Sprinkle with salt, pepper, and crushed Italian seasoning.

2 On charcoal grill, cook mushrooms on rack of uncovered grill directly over medium coals for 6 to 8 minutes, turning once halfway through cooking. Top each mushroom with a cheese slice. Place rolls, split sides down, on grill rack. Grill for 2 minutes more, until cheese is melted, mushrooms are tender, and rolls are toasted.

3 Serve mushrooms on rolls. Pass mayonnaise, sweet pepper pieces, and basil leaves at the table.

Nutrition facts per burger: 520 cal., 29 g total fat (9 g sat. fat), 25 mg chol., 972 mg sodium, 49 g carb., 17 g protein.

italian BREAD

Prep: 15 minutes
Rise: 1 hour 45 minutes
Stand: 10 minutes
Bake: 40 minutes
Oven: 375°F
Makes: 2 loaves
(30 servings)

5½ to 6 cups all-purpose flour

2 packages active dry yeast

1½ teaspoons salt

2 cups warm water (120°F
to 130°F)

Cornmeal

1 egg white, beaten lightly

1 tablespoon water

¼ teaspoon dried rosemary
or basil, crushed, or
⅛ teaspoon onion
powder or garlic powder
(optional)

1 In a large bowl, combine 2 cups of the flour, the yeast, and salt. Add the 2 cups warm water. Beat with an electric mixer on low speed for 30 seconds, scraping bowl. Beat on high speed for 3 minutes. Using a wooden spoon, stir in as much of the remaining flour as you can.

2 On a floured surface, knead in enough remaining flour to make a stiff dough that is smooth and elastic (8 to 10 minutes total). Shape into a ball. Place dough in a greased bowl; turn once to grease surface. Cover and let rise in a warm place until double (1 to 1½ hours).

3 Punch dough down. Divide in half. Cover; let rest for 10 minutes. Grease two baking sheets; sprinkle with cornmeal. On a lightly floured surface, roll each dough half into a 15x12-inch rectangle. Roll up from long side; seal well. Taper ends.

4 Place seam side down on prepared baking sheets. Brush with a mixture of egg white, the 1 tablespoon water, and, if desired, an herb or onion or garlic powder. Cover and let rise until nearly double (about 45 minutes). Make 5 or 6 diagonal cuts, ¼ inch deep, across tops.

5 Preheat oven to 375°F. Bake bread for 20 minutes. Brush again with the egg white mixture. Bake for 20 to 25 minutes more or until bread sound shallow when tapped. Cool on a wire rack.

Nutrition facts per serving: 80 cal., 0 g total fat (0 g sat. fat), 0 mg chol., 109 mg sodium, 17 g carb., 3 g protein.

Breadsticks: Divide each half of dough into 15 pieces. Roll each piece into an 8-inch rope. Place ropes on prepared baking sheets. Cover and let rise until nearly double (about 30 minutes). Brush with the egg white mixture. Bake for 10 minutes. Brush again with egg white mixture. Reduce oven temperature to 300°F and bake for 20 to 25 minutes more or until golden. Cool. Makes 30 breadsticks.

olive-arugula FLATBREAD

Start to Finish: 25 minutes
Makes: 4 servings

- 2 to 3 tablespoons olive oil
- 1 teaspoon lemon juice
- 1 teaspoon red wine vinegar
- ¼ teaspoon salt
- ⅛ teaspoon cracked black pepper
- 2 cups baby arugula leaves
- 1 14x12-inch Italian flatbread (focaccia), or one 12-inch thin Italian bread shell
- 2 teaspoons olive oil
- ¼ cup purchased olive pesto or tapenade
- 18 to 20 pimiento-stuffed green olives
- ¼ cup shaved Parmesan cheese (1 ounce)*

1 For dressing, in a screw-top jar, combine 2 to 3 tablespoons oil, lemon juice, vinegar, salt, and pepper. Cover and shake well. Place arugula in a medium bowl. Drizzle with dressing; toss gently to coat.

2 Brush flatbread with 2 teaspoons oil. For a charcoal grill, grill flatbread on the rack of an uncovered grill directly over medium coals for 1 to 2 minutes or just until golden brown, turning once halfway through grilling. (For a gas grill, preheat grill. Reduce heat to medium. Place flatbread on grill rack over heat. Cover and grill as above.)

3 Spread flatbread with pesto. Top with dressed arugula, olives, and cheese.

Nutrition facts per serving: 472 cal., 26 g total fat (6 g sat. fat), 4 mg chol., 879 mg sodium, 50 g carb., 12 g protein.

*Note: To shave the cheese, use a vegetable peeler or a grater with large slicing holes.

sheet pan FOCACCIA

Prep: 45 minutes
Rise: 1 hour 15 minutes
Chill: 16 to 24 hours
Bake: 19 minutes
Oven: 450°F
Makes: 16 to 24 servings

2⅓ to 3 cups all-purpose flour

1 package active dry yeast

2 teaspoons dried Italian seasoning, crushed

1 teaspoon salt

1¼ cups warm water (120°F to 130°F)

2 tablespoons olive oil

½ cup semolina flour
   Nonstick cooking spray

2 tablespoons olive oil

2 cups coarsely chopped onions

1 teaspoon packed brown sugar

¼ teaspoon salt

1 tablespoon fresh sage leaves, or 1 teaspoon dried sage

① In a large bowl, combine 1½ cups of the all-purpose flour, the yeast, Italian seasoning, and the 1 teaspoon salt. Add the water and 2 tablespoons oil. Beat with an electric mixer on low to medium speed for 30 seconds, scraping side of bowl constantly. Beat on high speed for 3 minutes. Using a wooden spoon, stir in semolina flour and as much of the remaining all-purpose flour as you can.

② Turn dough out onto a lightly floured surface. Knead in enough of the remaining all-purpose flour to make a moderately soft dough that is smooth and elastic (3 to 5 minutes total). Shape dough into a ball. Place in a lightly greased bowl, turning once to grease surface. Cover; let rise in a warm place until double in size (45 to 60 minutes).

③ Coat the inside of a large resealable plastic bag with cooking spray. Punch dough down. Place dough inside bag; seal bag, allowing room for dough to rise. Chill for 16 to 24 hours.

④ Grease a 15x10x1-inch baking pan. Remove dough from bag; place in the prepared baking pan. Gently pull and stretch dough into a 15x8-inch rectangle, being careful not to overwork dough. Lightly coat dough with cooking spray. Cover loosely with plastic wrap; let rise in a warm place until nearly double in size (about 45 minutes).

⑤ Preheat oven to 450°F. In a medium skillet, heat 2 tablespoons oil over medium-low heat. Add onions; cover and cook for 10 minutes, stirring frequently. Increase heat to medium-high. Stir in brown sugar and the ¼ teaspoon salt. Cook, uncovered, for 4 to 5 minutes more or until lightly browned, stirring frequently.

⑥ Using the tips of your fingers, press deep indentations into the surface of the dough every 1½ to 2 inches. Bake for about 15 minutes or until lightly browned.

⑦ Spread onion mixture over top of focaccia. Sprinkle randomly with fresh or dried sage; press gently into focaccia. Bake for 4 to 5 minutes more or until golden brown. Cool slightly. Cut into rectangles. Serve warm.

Nutrition facts per serving: 124 cal., 4 g total fat (1 g sat. fat), 0 mg chol., 184 mg sodium, 20 g carb., 3 g protein.

Tip: To bake the bread at once, prepare as directed through Step 2. Punch dough down; let rest for 10 minutes. Continue as directed in Step 4, except decrease rising time to 30 minutes.

bruschetta BISCUITS WITH FETA

Prep: 30 minutes
Bake: 15 minutes
Oven: 425°F
Makes: 9 biscuits

¾ **cup milk**

⅓ **cup olive oil**

1 **cup fresh baby spinach
    leaves, chopped**

¼ **cup fresh basil leaves,
    chopped**

¼ **cup dried tomatoes (not
    oil packed), chopped**

¼ **cup pitted Kalamata
    olives, chopped**

2 **cups all-purpose flour**

2 **teaspoons baking powder**

½ **teaspoon salt**

3 **tablespoons crumbled
    feta cheese**

1 **tablespoon pine nuts**

1 Preheat oven to 425°F. Line a baking sheet with parchment paper. In a bowl, combine milk, oil, spinach, basil, tomatoes, and olives. In a large bowl, combine flour, baking powder, and salt. Make a well in center of flour mixture. Add milk mixture all at once; with a fork stir until moistened.

2 Gently knead dough on a lightly floured surface until dough holds together. Pat into an 8-inch square. Cut into 9 squares.

3 Place biscuits 1 inch apart on prepared baking sheet. Brush lightly with milk. Sprinkle with feta cheese and pine nuts. Bake for 15 minutes or until golden. Cool slightly before serving.

Nutrition facts per biscuit: 210 cal., 11 g total fat (2 g sat. fat), 5 mg chol., 332 mg sodium, 24 g carb., 5 g protein.

Make-Ahead Directions: Store cooled biscuits in an airtight container in the refrigerator for up to 3 days. Reheat biscuits, wrapped in foil, in 350°F oven for 12 minutes.

Italian DOUGHNUTS

Cook: 2½ to 3 minutes per batch
Makes: 3 dozen doughnuts

1 **15-ounce container ricotta cheese**

4 **eggs**

1 **tablespoon vanilla**

1½ **cups all-purpose flour**

½ **cup granulated sugar**

2 **tablespoons baking powder**

½ **teaspoon salt**

Cooking oil for frying

Sifted powdered sugar or granulated sugar or cinnamon-sugar

In a large bowl, beat ricotta cheese with an electric mixer on medium speed until smooth. Add eggs and vanilla; beat until combined. Add flour, granulated sugar, baking powder, and salt. Beat on low speed until just combined. Let batter stand for 30 minutes. Drop batter by well-rounded teaspoonfuls, four or five at a time, into deep hot fat (365°F). Cook 2½ to 3 minutes or until golden brown, turning once. Remove doughnuts with slotted spoon and drain on paper towels. Repeat with remaining batter. Cool completely. Shake doughnuts in a bag with powdered sugar, granulated sugar, or cinnamon-sugar mixture.

Nutrition facts per doughnut: 102 cal., 6 g total fat (2 g sat. fat), 30 mg chol., 107 mg sodium, 9 g carb., 3 g protein.

pasta

Pasta with Bolognese Sauce, page 160

shells WITH WHITE BEANS AND BEEF

Prep: 10 minutes
Cook: 22 minutes
Makes: 8 servings

1 **tablespoon olive oil**

1 **pound beef fillet, cut into 1-inch cubes**

¾ **teaspoon salt**

½ **small onion, finely chopped**

2 **stalks celery with leaves, finely chopped**

3 **cloves garlic, finely chopped**

1 **28-ounce can crushed tomatoes**

2 **15-ounce cans cannellini beans, drained and rinsed**

½ **teaspoon dried oregano**

½ **teaspoon dried basil**

¼ **teaspoon red pepper flakes**

1 **pound medium shells**
  Grated cheese (optional)

1 Heat oil in a large nonstick lidded skillet over medium-high heat. Season beef with ¼ teaspoon of the salt. Add to skillet and cook for 2 minutes. Turn and cook for an additional 2 minutes. Remove beef from skillet to a plate with a slotted spoon. Keep warm.

2 Add onion and celery to skillet and cook, stirring occasionally, for 5 minutes. Add garlic and cook for 1 minute. Stir in tomatoes, beans, oregano, basil, red pepper flakes, and remaining ½ teaspoon salt. Bring to a boil. Reduce heat to medium-low and simmer, covered, for 12 minutes. Stir occasionally.

3 Meanwhile, cook pasta according to package directions. Drain, reserving 1 cup of the cooking water. Place drained pasta back into pot. Add the bean mixture, cooked beef with accumulated juices, and the reserved cooking water to the pasta.

4 Serve with grated cheese, if desired.

Nutrition facts per serving: 483 cal., 13 g total fat (5 g sat. fat), 37 mg chol., 545 mg sodium, 65 g carb., 25 g protein.

red PEPPER AND STEAK LINGUINE

Start to Finish: 25 minutes
Makes: 4 servings

- 1 **9-ounce package fresh linguine or fettuccine**
- 1 **cup fresh pea pods**
- 6 **ounces deli roast beef, sliced ¼ inch thick**
- ¼ **cup sour cream**
- 1½ **teaspoons all-purpose flour**
- 1 **cup bottled roasted red sweet peppers, drained**
- 2 **tablespoons purchased salsa**
- ½ **teaspoon sugar**
- ½ **cup chicken broth**

1 Cook pasta and pea pods together according to pasta package directions; drain. Return pasta mixture to hot pan; cover and keep warm. Meanwhile, cut meat into bite-size pieces. In a small bowl, combine sour cream and flour; set aside.

2 For sauce, in a food processor or blender, combine roasted peppers, salsa, and sugar. Cover and process or blend until nearly smooth. Transfer mixture to a small saucepan. Stir in broth.

3 Cook and stir over medium heat until bubbly. Stir in sour cream mixture. Cook and stir for 1 minute more. Stir in meat; heat through. Pour sauce over pasta mixture; toss gently to coat.

Nutrition facts per serving: 394 cal., 8 g total fat (4 g sat. fat), 89 mg chol., 877 mg sodium, 56 g carb., 24 g protein.

fusilli WITH CREAMY TOMATO AND MEAT SAUCE

Whipping cream enriches this herbed tomato and meat sauce served over pasta.

Prep: 20 minutes
Cook: 40 minutes
Makes: 4 servings

- 12 ounces lean ground beef or ground turkey
- 1 large onion, chopped
- 2 cloves garlic, minced
- 2 14.5-ounce cans Italian-style tomatoes, cut up
- 1 teaspoon dried Italian seasoning, crushed
- ½ teaspoon sugar
- ¼ teaspoon salt
- ⅛ teaspoon ground black pepper
- 8 ounces fusilli, vermicelli, or spaghetti
- ½ cup whipping cream
- 2 tablespoon snipped fresh parsley
  Fresh rosemary sprigs (optional)

1 For sauce, in a large saucepan, cook ground meat, onion, and garlic until meat is brown. Drain off fat. Stir in undrained tomatoes, Italian seasoning, sugar, salt, and pepper. Bring to boiling; reduce heat. Simmer, uncovered, for about 40 minutes or until most of the liquid is evaporated, stirring occasionally.

2 Meanwhile, cook pasta according to package directions; drain. Return to saucepan; cover and keep warm.

3 Gradually stir the whipping cream into the sauce. Heat through, stirring constantly. Remove from heat. Stir in parsley.

4 Transfer cooked pasta to dinner plates or a warm serving platter. Spoon the sauce over pasta. If desired, garnish with fresh rosemary.

Nutrition facts per serving: 512 cal., 20 g total fat (10 g sat. fat), 95 mg chol., 496 mg sodium, 57 g carb., 26 g protein.

one-pot SPAGHETTI

This easy spaghetti recipe lets you cook the pasta right in the tomato sauce, so there's less fuss and less cleanup.

Start to Finish: 40 minutes
Makes: 4 servings

8 ounces ground beef or bulk pork sausage

1 cup sliced fresh mushrooms, or one 6-ounce jar sliced mushrooms, drained

½ cup chopped onion (1 medium)

1 clove garlic, minced

1 14-ounce can chicken broth or beef broth

1¾ cups water

1 6-ounce can tomato paste

1 teaspoon dried Italian seasoning

¼ teaspoon black pepper

6 ounces spaghetti, broken

¼ cup grated Parmesan cheese

1 In a large saucepan, cook the ground beef, fresh mushrooms (if using), onion, and garlic until meat is brown and onion is tender. Drain.

2 Stir in the canned mushrooms (if using), broth, water, tomato paste, Italian seasoning, and pepper. Bring to boiling. Add the broken spaghetti, a little at a time, stirring constantly. Return to boiling; reduce heat. Boil gently, uncovered, for 17 to 20 minutes or until spaghetti is tender and sauce is desired consistency, stirring frequently. Serve with Parmesan cheese.

Nutrition facts per serving: 394 cal., 15 g total fat (6 g sat. fat), 39 mg chol., 926 mg sodium, 44 g carb., 22 g protein.

saucy RAVIOLI WITH MEATBALLS

Three of the all-time-best Italian convenience products—spaghetti sauce, frozen ravioli, and frozen Italian meatballs—make this a super-speedy dish to prepare.

Prep: 20 minutes
Cook: 4½ to 5 hours (low)
      or 2½ to 3 hours
      (high)
Stand: 15 minutes
Makes: 10 to 12 servings

2 **26-ounce jars spaghetti sauce with mushrooms and onions**

2 **24-ounce packages frozen ravioli**

1 **12-ounce package frozen cooked Italian meatballs, thawed**

2 **cups shredded mozzarella cheese (8 ounces)**

½ **cup finely shredded Parmesan cheese**

1 Lightly coat a 5½- or 6-quart slow cooker with cooking spray. Add 1 cup of the spaghetti sauce. Add frozen ravioli from one package and the meatballs. Sprinkle with 1 cup of the mozzarella cheese. Top with remaining spaghetti sauce from first jar. Add ravioli from remaining package and remaining 1 cup mozzarella cheese. Pour spaghetti sauce from second jar over mixture in cooker.

2 Cover; cook on low-heat setting for 4½ to 5 hours or on high-heat setting for 2½ to 3 hours. Turn off cooker. Sprinkle ravioli mixture with Parmesan cheese. Cover; let stand for 15 minutes before serving.

Nutrition facts per serving: 510 cal., 18 g total fat (8 g sat. fat), 78 mg chol., 1551 mg sodium, 67 g carb., 26 g protein.

chicken AND PESTO LASAGNA

Prep: 10 minutes
Cook: 7 minutes
Cook: 5½ hours (low) or
      3 hours (high)
Makes: 6 servings

- 1 tablespoon canola oil
- 1 medium onion, chopped
- 2 garlic cloves, minced
- 1 pound ground chicken
- 1 10-ounce package frozen chopped spinach, thawed and squeezed dry
- ¼ cup reduced-fat pesto
- ½ teaspoon salt
- ¼ teaspoon ground black pepper
- 1 cup part-skim ricotta cheese
- ¾ cup Italian blend shredded cheese
- 10 lasagna noodles, broken in half
- ½ cup water

1 Heat oil in a large nonstick skillet over medium-high heat. Add onion and garlic to skillet and cook for 3 minutes or until softened. Add chicken to skillet and cook, stirring frequently, for about 4 minutes or until no longer pink. Add spinach, pesto, salt, and pepper to skillet and stir until well blended; set aside.

2 In a small bowl, combine ricotta and ½ cup of the Italian shredded cheese.

3 Coat slow cooker bowl with nonstick cooking spray, then layer one-third of the uncooked noodles, overlapping as necessary. Spread one-third of the chicken mixture over noodles, then top with ¼ cup of the water. Dollop one-third of the ricotta mixture on top, and continue layering with remaining noodles, meat, the remaining ¼ cup water, and ricotta mixture.

4 Cover and cook on low for 5½ hours or high for 3 hours. Sprinkle remaining ¼ cup of Italian cheese on top for last 15 minutes of cook time or until melted.

Nutrition facts per serving: 394 cal., 19 g total fat (8 g sat. fat), 144 mg chol., 547 mg sodium, 29 g carb., 28 g protein.

chicken ALFREDO CASSEROLE

Prep: 30 minutes
Bake: 25 minutes
Oven: 350°F
Makes: 6 servings

- 1 19-ounce package frozen cheese-filled tortellini
- 3 cloves garlic, minced
- 1 tablespoon olive oil
- 1 pound skinless, boneless chicken breast halves, cubed
- 1 cup chopped pepperoni
- ¾ cup oil-pack dried tomatoes, drained and chopped
- 1 15- to 16-ounce jar Alfredo pasta sauce
- ½ cup shredded Italian blend cheese (2 ounces)

  Chopped fresh parsley (optional)

1 Preheat oven to 350°F. Cook tortellini according to package directions; drain.

2 Meanwhile, in large skillet, cook garlic in hot oil for 15 seconds; add chicken. Cook, stirring occasionally, for 3 to 4 minutes or until no pink remains. Stir in pepperoni and tomatoes; cook for 2 minutes. Add Alfredo sauce; heat through.

3 In large bowl, combine tortellini and chicken mixture; transfer to 2-quart casserole. Sprinkle with cheese.

4 Bake, covered, for 25 to 30 minutes or until heated through. Sprinkle with parsley.

Nutrition facts per serving: 588 cal., 32 g total fat (15 g sat. fat), 130 mg chol., 1059 mg sodium, 42 g carb., 36 g protein.

chicken AND OLIVES

Start to Finish: 30 minutes
Makes: 6 to 8 servings

- **1 pound skinless, boneless chicken breast halves, cut into 1-inch pieces**
- **1 large onion, cut into thin wedges**
- **2 cloves garlic, minced**
- **2 tablespoons olive oil**
- **1 28-ounce can Italian-style whole peeled tomatoes in puree**
- **½ teaspoon coarsely ground black pepper**
- **¼ teaspoon salt**
- **½ cup whipping cream**
- **1½ cups large pimiento-stuffed green olives and/or pitted Kalamata or other Italian olives, sliced**
- **½ cup slivered fresh basil**
- **¼ cup grated Parmesan cheese**
- **12 to 16 ounces pasta, cooked and drained**

1 In a large skillet, cook chicken, onion, and garlic in hot oil over medium-high heat for 5 to 7 minutes or until chicken is no longer pink, stirring occasionally. Meanwhile, place half of the tomatoes in a blender or food processor. Cover and blend or process until smooth. Snip the remaining tomatoes into bite-size pieces.

2 Stir pureed tomatoes, tomato pieces in puree, pepper, and salt into chicken mixture. Bring to boiling; reduce heat. Boil gently, uncovered, for 2 minutes. Stir in cream. Boil gently, uncovered, for 3 minutes more, stirring occasionally. Stir in olives; heat through.

3 Add chicken mixture, basil, and cheese to hot cooked pasta; toss gently to combine.

Nutrition facts per serving: 499 cal., 20 g total fat (7 g sat. fat), 74 mg chol., 891 mg sodium, 53 g carb., 28 g protein.

easy CHICKEN TETRAZZINI

Legend has it that Chicken Tetrazzini was created for a famous opera singer—but that doesn't stop this dish from being wonderfully homey, crowd-pleasing fare!

Prep: 20 minutes
Cook: 5 to 6 hours (low) or 2½ to 3 hours (high)
Makes: 8 servings

2½ **pounds skinless, boneless chicken breast halves and/or thighs, cut into 1-inch pieces**

2 **4.5-ounce jars (drained weight) sliced mushrooms, drained**

1 **16-ounce jar Alfredo pasta sauce**

¼ **cup chicken broth or water**

2 **tablespoons dry sherry (optional)**

¼ **teaspoon ground black pepper**

¼ **teaspoon ground nutmeg**

10 **ounces spaghetti or linguine**

⅔ **cup grated Parmesan cheese**

¾ **cup thinly sliced scallions (6)**

Toasted French bread slices (optional)

1 In a 3½- or 4-quart slow cooker, combine chicken and mushrooms. In a medium bowl, stir together Alfredo sauce, broth, sherry (if desired), pepper, and nutmeg. Pour over chicken mixture in cooker.

2 Cover and cook on low-heat setting for 5 to 6 hours or on high-heat setting for 2½ to 3 hours.

3 Meanwhile, cook spaghetti according to package directions; drain. Stir Parmesan cheese into chicken mixture in cooker. Serve chicken mixture over spaghetti, topping each serving with scallions. If desired, serve with toasted French bread slices.

Nutrition facts per serving: 430 cal., 14 g total fat (6 g sat. fat), 121 mg chol., 753 mg sodium, 32 g carb., 42 g protein.

fast CHICKEN FETTUCCINE

Refrigerated pasta makes this zucchini and chicken dish even quicker to prepare.

Start to Finish: 20 minutes
Makes: 4 servings

1 **9-ounce package fresh fettuccine**

¼ **cup oil-pack dried tomato strips or pieces**

1 **large zucchini or yellow summer squash, halved lengthwise and sliced (about 2 cups)**

8 **ounces chicken breast strips**

½ **cup finely shredded Parmesan, Romano, or Asiago cheese (2 ounces)**

Ground black pepper

1 Use kitchen scissors to cut pasta in half. Cook pasta in lightly salted boiling water according to package directions; drain. Return pasta to hot pan.

2 Meanwhile, drain dried tomato, reserving 2 tablespoons oil from jar.

3 In a large skillet, heat 1 tablespoon reserved oil over medium-high heat. Add zucchini; cook and stir for 2 to 3 minutes or until crisp-tender. Remove from skillet. Add remaining reserved oil to skillet. Add chicken; cook and stir for 2 to 3 minutes or until no longer pink. Add zucchini, chicken, and tomato to cooked pasta; toss gently to combine. Sprinkle individual servings with cheese and season to taste with pepper.

Nutrition facts per serving: 381 cal., 14 g total fat (1 g sat. fat), 40 mg chol., 334 mg sodium, 40 g carb., 24 g protein.

chicken MANICOTTI WITH RED PEPPER CREAM SAUCE

Roasted red pepper, reduced-fat cream cheese, and skim milk combine to make a creamy sauce to spoon over chicken- and broccoli-filled manicotti.

Prep: 40 minutes
Bake: 30 minutes
Oven: 350°F
Makes: 6 servings

12 **manicotti or 18 conchiglioni (jumbo shells)**

1 **8-ounce package reduced-fat cream cheese, cut up**

¾ **cup fat-free milk**

½ **of a 7-ounce jar roasted red sweet peppers (about ½ cup), drained and chopped, or one 4-ounce jar diced pimiento, drained**

3 **tablespoons grated Parmesan cheese**

1 **9-ounce package frozen diced cooked chicken, thawed (2 cups)**

1 **10-ounce package frozen chopped broccoli, thawed and drained**

2 **tablespoons thinly sliced scallion**

¼ **teaspoon ground black pepper**

1 Cook pasta according to package directions. Rinse with cold water; drain well.

2 Preheat oven to 350°F. For sauce, in a heavy small saucepan stir cream cheese and ¼ cup of the milk over medium-low heat until smooth. Stir in remaining milk. Stir in sweet peppers or pimiento and Parmesan cheese; heat through.

3 For filling, in a large bowl stir together ¾ cup of the sauce (set remaining sauce aside), the chicken, broccoli, onion, and black pepper. Using a small spoon, stuff each tube with about ¼ cup of the filling or each shell with 2 to 3 tablespoons filling. Place in a 3-quart rectangular baking dish. Bake, covered, for 30 minutes or until heated through.

4 To serve, cook and stir remaining sauce over low heat until heated through. Place 2 manicotti or 3 shells on each serving plate. Spoon sauce over shells.

Nutrition facts per serving: 318 cal., 14 g total fat (7 g sat. fat), 76 mg chol., 291 mg sodium, 24 g carb., 23 g protein.

Test Kitchen Tip: When a recipe calls for cooked chicken, you can purchase a package of frozen diced cooked chicken (as called for here). Or, purchase a deli-roasted chicken. A cooked chicken will yield 1½ to 2 cups boneless chopped meat. If you have more time, you can poach chicken breast. For 2 cups cubed cooked chicken, in a large skillet place 12 ounces skinless, boneless chicken breasts and 1½ cups water. Bring to boiling; reduce heat. Cover and simmer for 12 to 14 minutes or until chicken is tender and no longer pink. Drain well. Cut up the chicken.

cavatappi WITH TOMATOES AND HAM

Start to Finish: 30 minutes
Makes: 4 servings

1 medium onion, cut into ¼-inch slices

12 red and/or yellow cherry and/or pear tomatoes, halved

8 ounces cavatappi or gemelli

¼ teaspoon crushed red pepper (optional)

2 ounces thinly sliced cooked ham, cut into strips

3 tablespoons thinly sliced fresh basil

2 tablespoons garlic-flavored olive oil or olive oil

1 Preheat broiler. Place onion slices on foil-lined rack of an unheated broiler pan. Broil onion slices 4 inches from heat for 5 minutes. Add tomato halves to pan; broil for about 5 minutes more or until edges are brown.

2 Meanwhile, cook pasta according to package directions, adding crushed red pepper (if desired) to water. Drain well. Return pasta to pan; cover and keep warm.

3 Cut up onion slices. Toss onion pieces and tomato halves with pasta, ham, basil, and olive oil.

Nutrition facts per serving: 341 cal., 11 g total fat (2 g sat. fat), 16 mg chol., 381 mg sodium, 47 g carb., 13 g protein.

lemony PORK AND PECORINO MEATBALLS

Prep: 35 minutes
Cook: 12 minutes
Makes: 4 servings

1   egg, lightly beaten
⅔   cup grated Pecorino
    Romano cheese
½   cup fine dry bread crumbs
¼   cup snipped fresh flat-leaf
    parsley
2   teaspoons finely
    shredded lemon peel
2   teaspoons snipped fresh
    rosemary
4   cloves garlic, minced
½   teaspoon salt
12 ounces lean ground pork
3   tablespoons all-purpose
    flour
3   tablespoons olive oil
¾   cup dry white wine
2   cups water
1   bay leaf
¼   teaspoon salt
1   cup orzo (rosamarina)
1   tablespoon lemon juice
    Lemon wedges

1 In a large bowl, combine egg, cheese, bread crumbs, parsley, lemon peel, rosemary, garlic, and the ½ teaspoon salt. Add ground pork; mix well. Shape mixture into 24 meatballs. Place flour in a shallow dish. Roll meatballs in flour to coat.

2 In a very large skillet, heat oil over medium heat. Add meatballs; cook for 5 to 7 minutes or until browned, turning occasionally. Remove from heat.

3 Add wine to skillet; shake skillet slightly to distribute meatballs evenly. Bring to boiling; reduce heat. Simmer, uncovered, for 3 minutes. Add the water, bay leaf, and the ¼ teaspoon salt. Return to boiling. Stir in orzo, making sure it is covered by liquid; reduce heat. Cover and simmer for about 9 minutes or until orzo is tender, stirring once or twice. Discard bay leaf.

4 Stir lemon juice into meatball mixture. Serve with lemon wedges.

Nutrition facts per serving: 532 cal., 23 g total fat (7 g sat. fat), 107 mg chol., 1013 mg sodium, 49 g carb., 24 g protein.

tuscan MAC 'N' CHEESE

Prep: 45 minutes
Bake: 50 minutes
Stand: 15 minutes
Oven: 350°F
Makes: 6 to 8 servings

8 **ounces sweet or hot Italian sausage**

8 **ounces gemelli or elbow macaroni, cooked and drained**

1 **8-ounce package cream cheese, cut into cubes and softened**

4 **ounces crusty Italian bread, cut into 1-inch cubes (about 2 cups)**

1 **cup pitted Kalamata olives, halved**

1 **cup shredded mozzarella cheese (4 ounces)**

1 **tablespoon butter**

1 **tablespoon all-purpose flour**

1 **tablespoon snipped fresh sage, or 1 teaspoon dried leaf sage, crushed**

1 **teaspoon snipped fresh thyme, or ¼ teaspoon dried thyme, crushed**

½ **teaspoon salt**

⅛ **teaspoon cayenne pepper**

1½ **cups milk**

1 **medium tomato, sliced**

½ **cup shredded Asiago, Parmesan, or Romano cheese (2 ounces)**

1 Preheat oven to 350°F. Remove casings, if present, from sausage. In a skillet, cook and crumble sausage; drain. In a very large bowl, combine sausage, cooked pasta, cream cheese, bread cubes, olives, and mozzarella cheese.

2 In a medium saucepan, melt butter over medium heat. Stir in flour, sage, thyme, salt, and cayenne pepper. Add milk all at once. Cook and stir until slightly thickened and bubbly. Pour sauce over pasta mixture. Stir gently.

3 Transfer mixture to a 2-quart casserole. Bake, covered, for 35 minutes. Uncover; top with tomato slices and Asiago cheese. Bake, uncovered, for 15 minutes more or until heated through. Let stand for 15 minutes before serving. Sprinkle with additional fresh thyme, if desired.

Nutrition facts per serving: 637 cal., 39 g total fat (19 g sat. fat), 101 mg chol., 1187 mg sodium, 46 g carb., 24 g protein.

pasta WITH BOLOGNESE SAUCE

Prep: 40 minutes
Cook: 30 minutes
Makes: 6 servings

- 12 ounces pasta, such as spaghetti, linguine, or penne
- 1 pound bulk sweet Italian sausage or ground beef
- 1 cup chopped onion (1 large)
- ½ cup finely chopped carrot (1 medium)
- ½ cup chopped green sweet pepper (½ large)
- ¼ cup chopped celery
- 4 cloves garlic, minced
- 2 pounds roma tomatoes, peeled (if desired), seeded, and chopped (about 4 cups), or two 14.5-ounce cans diced tomatoes, undrained
- 1 6-ounce can tomato paste
- ½ cup dry red wine or beef broth
- 2 tablespoons snipped fresh basil, or 1½ teaspoons dried basil, crushed
- 1 tablespoon snipped fresh oregano, or 1 teaspoon dried oregano, crushed
- 2 teaspoons snipped fresh marjoram, or ½ teaspoon dried marjoram, crushed
- ½ teaspoon salt
- ¼ teaspoon ground black pepper
- ¼ cup whipping cream
- 2 tablespoons snipped fresh Italian parsley

1 In a large saucepan, cook pasta according to package directions. Drain; keep warm.

2 Meanwhile, in a large pot, cook sausage, onion, carrot, sweet pepper, celery, and garlic until meat is brown and onion is tender. Drain.

3 Stir in tomatoes, tomato paste, wine, dried herbs (if using), salt, and black pepper. Bring to boiling; reduce heat. Simmer, covered, for 30 minutes, stirring occasionally. If necessary, uncover and simmer for 10 minutes more or to desired consistency, stirring occasionally. Stir in whipping cream, parsley, and fresh herbs (if using); heat through. Serve sauce over hot pasta.

Nutrition facts per serving: 570 cal., 22 g total fat (10 g sat. fat), 66 mg chol., 652 mg sodium, 60 g carb., 22 g protein.

lasagna

Prep: 30 minutes
Cook: 15 minutes
Bake: 30 minutes
Stand: 10 minutes
Oven: 375°F
Makes: 12 servings

9 dried lasagna noodles

1 pound bulk Italian sausage
  or ground beef

1 cup chopped onion (1 large)

2 cloves garlic, minced

1 14.5-ounce can diced
  tomatoes, undrained

1 8-ounce can tomato sauce

2 to 3 tablespoons snipped
  fresh rosemary, oregano,
  and/or parsley, or 1
  tablespoon dried Italian
  seasoning, crushed

1 teaspoon fennel seeds,
  crushed (optional)

¼ teaspoon ground black
  pepper

1 egg, lightly beaten

1 15-ounce carton ricotta
  cheese, or 2 cups cream-
  style cottage cheese,
  drained

¼ cup grated Parmesan
  cheese

8 ounces fresh mozzarella
  cheese, sliced, or 2 cups
  shredded mozzarella
  cheese (8 ounces)

Grated Parmesan cheese
(optional)

Fresh rosemary, oregano,
and/or parsley sprigs
(optional)

1 Preheat oven to 375°F. Cook lasagna noodles according to package directions; drain. Rinse with cold water; drain again. Place lasagna noodles in a single layer on a sheet of foil.

2 Meanwhile, for meat sauce, in a large skillet, cook sausage, onion, and garlic over medium-high heat until meat is brown; drain off fat. Stir in undrained tomatoes, tomato sauce, snipped herbs, fennel seeds (if desired), and pepper. Bring to boiling; reduce heat. Simmer, covered, for 15 minutes, stirring occasionally.

3 For filling, in a medium bowl, combine egg, ricotta cheese, and ¼ cup Parmesan cheese.

4 Spread about ¼ cup of the meat sauce over the bottom of an ungreased 3-quart rectangular baking dish. Layer three of the cooked lasagna noodles in dish. Spread with one-third of the filling and one-third of the remaining meat sauce. Top with one-third of the mozzarella cheese. Repeat layering noodles, filling, meat sauce, and mozzarella cheese two more times (make sure the top layer of noodles is completely covered with meat sauce). If desired, sprinkle with additional Parmesan cheese.

5 Bake, uncovered, for 30 to 35 minutes or until heated through. Let stand for 10 minutes before serving. If desired, garnish with herb sprigs.

Nutrition facts per serving: 340 cal., 22 g total fat (10 g sat. fat), 79 mg chol., 563 mg sodium, 18 g carb., 17 g protein.

Make-Ahead Directions: Prepare as directed through Step 4. Cover unbaked lasagna; chill for 2 to 24 hours. To serve, preheat oven to 375°F. Bake, covered, for 40 minutes. Bake, uncovered, for about 20 minutes more or until heated through. Let stand for 10 minutes before serving.

italian PENNE BAKE

This homey casserole contains many of the most popular pizza ingredients—marinara sauce, mushrooms, onion, green sweet pepper, pepperoni, and lots of cheese.

Prep: 25 minutes
Bake: 30 minutes
Oven: 350°F
Makes: 4 servings

1½ cups penne

 1 medium green or red sweet pepper, cut into thin, bite-size strips

 3 ounces sliced pepperoni or Canadian-style bacon, cut up

 ½ cup sliced fresh mushrooms

 ½ cup quartered, thinly sliced onion

1½ teaspoons bottled minced garlic (3 cloves)

1½ teaspoons olive oil or cooking oil

1½ cups marinara sauce

 ⅔ cup shredded Italian blend cheese

1 Preheat oven to 350°F. Lightly coat a 2-quart square baking dish with nonstick cooking spray. Cook pasta according to package directions; drain well. Return pasta to saucepan. Meanwhile, in a medium skillet, cook sweet pepper, pepperoni, mushrooms, onion, and garlic in hot oil for 3 minutes. Add vegetable mixture and marinara sauce to pasta; toss to coat. Spread pasta mixture evenly in prepared baking dish.

2 Bake, covered, for about 25 minutes or until heated through. Uncover and sprinkle with cheese. Bake, uncovered, for about 5 minutes more or until cheese is melted.

Nutrition facts per serving: 390 cal., 19 g total fat (7 g sat. fat), 31 mg chol., 848 mg sodium, 41 g carb., 15 g protein.

gnocchi IN PARMESAN CREAM SAUCE WITH PEAS

Start to Finish: 1 hour
Makes: 6 servings

- 2 **pounds russet potatoes**
- 3 **eggs**
- 1 **cup all-purpose flour**
- ½ **cup whipping cream**
- ½ **cup frozen peas, thawed**
- ½ **teaspoon salt**
- ½ **teaspoon ground white pepper**
- 4 **ounces thinly sliced prosciutto, cut into ¼-inch-thick strips**
- ¼ **cup grated Parmigiano-Reggiano cheese**
- 3 **tablespoons butter**
  Freshly grated Parmigiano-Reggiano cheese (optional)

1 In a covered 8-quart Dutch oven or pot, cook potatoes in enough boiling water to cover for about 20 minutes or just until tender (do not overcook); drain. Peel potatoes.

2 While potatoes are still hot, push through a ricer into a large bowl. Using a wooden spoon, stir in eggs one at a time, mixing well after each addition. Add about half of the flour; mix well. Stir in enough of the remaining flour to make a soft, pliable dough. Divide dough in thirds.

3 On a lightly floured surface, roll one portion of the dough at a time into a 1-inch-thick rope. Cut rope into ½-inch pieces. Using your thumb, make an indentation in top of each piece. Place on a baking sheet; chill while preparing the sauce (up to 2 hours).

4 For sauce, in a medium saucepan, heat whipping cream over medium heat. Stir in peas, salt, and pepper. Simmer gently for 3 minutes. Stir in prosciutto and the ¼ cup cheese; simmer gently for 1 minute more. Stir in butter until melted. Remove from heat; cover and keep warm.

5 In the Dutch oven or pot, bring 6 quarts salted water to a rapid boil. Add half of the gnocchi; cook for 10 to 15 seconds or until gnocchi start to float. Using a slotted spoon, transfer to a warm serving bowl. Repeat with the remaining gnocchi.

6 Pour sauce over gnocchi; stir gently to coat. If desired, sprinkle with additional cheese.

Nutrition facts per serving: 429 cal., 22 g total fat (10 g sat. fat), 151 mg chol., 683 mg sodium, 45 g carb., 15 g protein.

arugula–dried tomato PASTA

Start to Finish: 30 minutes
Makes: 6 to 8 servings

1 **cup sliced shallots (8 medium)**

4 **cloves garlic, minced**

2 **tablespoons olive oil**

1 **8-ounce jar oil-pack dried tomatoes, drained and cut into thin strips**

6 **to 8 ounces Genoa salami, cut into ½-inch pieces**

½ **cup dry white wine**

1 **cup chicken broth**

5 **ounces baby arugula**

1½ **cups crumbled ricotta salata cheese (6 ounces)**

⅔ **cup chopped walnuts, toasted**

2 **tablespoons assorted snipped fresh herbs (such as Italian parsley, oregano, marjoram, and/ or thyme)**

¼ **teaspoon ground black pepper**

Salt (optional)

12 **to 16 ounces pasta, cooked and drained**

❶ In an extra-large skillet, cook and stir shallots and garlic in hot oil over medium heat for about 4 minutes or until tender. Add dried tomatoes and salami; cook and stir for 1 minute. Carefully add wine. Bring to boiling; reduce heat. Boil gently, uncovered, for 3 to 4 minutes or until wine is nearly evaporated.

❷ Add broth to tomato mixture. Return to boiling; reduce heat. Boil gently, uncovered, for 1 to 2 minutes or until slightly reduced. Stir in arugula, 1 cup of the ricotta salata, the walnuts, herbs, and pepper. Cook and stir just until arugula is wilted. If desired, season to taste with salt.

❸ Serve tomato mixture over hot cooked pasta. Top with the remaining ½ cup ricotta salata.

Nutrition facts per serving: 463 cal., 35 g total fat (6 g sat. fat), 54 mg chol., 1270 mg sodium, 58 g carb., 23 g protein.

angel HAIR WITH ARUGULA PESTO AND SALMON

Prep: 10 minutes
Cook: 10 minutes
Makes: 8 servings

- 2 **cups baby arugula leaves**
- ¾ **cup basil leaves**
- ½ **cup toasted hazelnuts**
- 2 **cloves garlic, peeled**
- ⅔ **cup extra virgin olive oil**
- ⅔ **cup grated Parmesan cheese**
- 1¼ **teaspoons salt**
- 1¼ **pounds salmon fillet**
- 1 **cup dry white wine or vegetable broth**
- 1 **pound angel hair pasta**

❶ For pesto, in food processor, combine arugula, basil, nuts, and garlic. Process for 1 minute. Gradually add oil and process until blended. Add cheese and salt; process until smooth. Set aside 1 cup for recipe. Refrigerate remainder for another use (up to 1 week).

❷ Place salmon fillet in a large nonstick skillet. Add wine and bring to a boil over medium-high heat. Reduce heat to medium-low and simmer, covered, for 10 minutes or until fish flakes easily. Remove from poaching liquid; keep warm. Discard liquid.

❸ Meanwhile, cook pasta according to package directions. Drain, reserving ½ cup of the water. Toss drained pasta with 1 cup pesto and ¼ cup of the pasta water, adding more water if needed. Remove skin from salmon; discard. Flake fish into pasta.

Nutrition facts per serving: 530 cal., 25 g total fat (4 g sat. fat), 48 mg chol., 500 mg sodium, 43 g carb., 27 g protein.

linguine WITH SHRIMP AND PINE NUTS

This dish will transport you to Italy's ocean-side region of Liguria, where linguine originates. Linguine actually means "little tongues" in Italian.

Start to Finish: 35 minutes
Makes: 4 servings

- 12 **ounces fresh or frozen medium shrimp in shells**
- 8 **ounces linguine**
- ¾ **cup chicken broth**
- ⅓ **cup dry sherry or chicken broth**
- 2 **tablespoons lemon juice**
- ¼ **teaspoon salt**
- ¼ **teaspoon crushed red pepper**
- ¼ **cup pine nuts**
- 2 **cloves garlic, minced**
- 1 **tablespoon olive oil**
- 4 **ounces fresh mushrooms (such as button, cremini, and/or shiitake), sliced**
- 1 **tablespoon butter**
- 4 **cups fresh baby spinach**
- ¼ **cup grated Asiago cheese**
   Pine nuts, toasted (optional)

1 Thaw shrimp, if frozen. Peel and devein shrimp, leaving tails intact (if desired). Rinse shrimp; pat dry with paper towels. In a Dutch oven, cook linguine according to package directions; drain. Return linguine to hot pan; cover and keep warm.

2 Meanwhile, in a small bowl, combine broth, sherry, lemon juice, salt, and crushed red pepper; set aside.

3 In a large skillet, cook shrimp, ¼ cup pine nuts, and garlic in hot oil over medium heat for 2 to 3 minutes or until shrimp are opaque, stirring frequently. Remove shrimp mixture from skillet.

4 Add mushrooms and butter to skillet. Cook for about 3 minutes or until mushrooms are nearly tender, stirring occasionally. Carefully add broth mixture. Bring to boiling; reduce heat. Boil gently, uncovered, for 5 minutes. Return shrimp mixture to skillet; heat through.

5 To serve, divide warm linguine among shallow bowls. Top with shrimp mixture, spinach, cheese, and (if desired) additional pine nuts.

Nutrition facts per serving: 492 cal., 17 g total fat (5 g sat. fat), 145 mg chol., 577 mg sodium, 50 g carb., 31 g protein.

broccoli RAAB AND CLAMS

Start to Finish: 25 minutes
Makes: 6 to 8 servings

1 **pound broccoli raab, trimmed and cut into 2-inch pieces, or 3 cups broccoli florets**

3 **cloves garlic, sliced**

2 **tablespoons olive oil**

2 **6.5-ounce cans chopped clams, undrained**

¼ **cup butter**

½ **cup dry white wine**

½ **teaspoon crushed red pepper**

¼ **teaspoon ground black pepper**

12 **to 16 ounces pasta, cooked and drained**

¼ **cup grated Parmesan cheese**

1 In an extra-large skillet, cook broccoli and garlic in hot oil over medium-high heat for 5 minutes, stirring occasionally. Stir in undrained clams and butter. Cook over medium heat until butter is melted.

2 Stir in wine, crushed red pepper, and black pepper. Bring just to boiling; reduce heat. Simmer, uncovered, for about 2 minutes or until slightly reduced.

3 Serve broccoli mixture over hot cooked pasta. Sprinkle with cheese.

Nutrition facts per serving: 469 cal., 15 g total fat (6 g sat. fat), 64 mg chol., 219 mg sodium, 49 g carb., 27 g protein.

aglio E OLIO

Start to Finish: 20 minutes
Makes: 6 servings

½ **cup olive oil**

8 **cloves garlic, minced**

½ **to 1 teaspoon crushed red pepper**

½ **cup finely shredded Pecorino Romano cheese (2 ounces)**

⅓ **cup snipped fresh Italian (flat-leaf) parsley**

½ **teaspoon ground black pepper**

¼ **teaspoon salt**

12 **to 16 ounces pasta, cooked and drained**

Finely shredded Pecorino Romano cheese

1 In a small saucepan, heat oil over medium heat. Add garlic and crushed red pepper; cook for about 1 minute or until fragrant. Remove from heat.

2 Add garlic mixture, ½ cup cheese, parsley, black pepper, and salt to hot cooked pasta; toss gently to coat. Serve with additional cheese.

Nutrition facts per serving: 409 cal., 21 g total fat (4 g sat. fat), 9 mg chol., 203 mg sodium, 44 g carb., 10 g protein.

farfalle WITH SPINACH AND MUSHROOMS

In Italy, bow-tie pasta is called farfalle, which means "butterfly." Here it combines with fresh mushrooms to create a pasta dish that tastes as alluring as it looks.

Start to Finish: 25 minutes
Makes: 4 side-dish servings

- 6 **ounces bow-tie pasta**
- 1 **tablespoon butter or margarine**
- 1 **medium onion, chopped**
- 1 **cup sliced portobello or other fresh mushrooms (such as chanterelles, shiitakes, and/or cremini)**
- 2 **cloves garlic, minced**
- 4 **cups thinly sliced fresh spinach**
- 1 **teaspoon snipped fresh thyme**
- ⅛ **teaspoon ground black pepper**
- 1 **tablespoon licorice-flavored liqueur (optional)**
- 2 **tablespoons finely shredded Parmesan cheese**

1 Cook pasta according to package directions; drain well.

2 Meanwhile, in a large skillet, melt butter or margarine over medium heat. Add onion, mushrooms, and garlic; cook and stir for 2 to 3 minutes or until mushrooms are nearly tender.

3 Stir in spinach, thyme, and pepper; cook for 1 minute or until heated through and spinach is slightly wilted.

4 Stir in cooked pasta and, if desired, liqueur; toss gently to mix. Sprinkle with cheese.

Nutrition facts per serving: 220 cal., 5 g total fat (3 g sat. fat), 10 mg chol., 105 mg sodium, 36 g carb., 9 g protein.

pasta PRIMAVERA

Prep: 20 minutes
Cook: 14 minutes
Makes: 6 servings

8 ounces asparagus,
  trimmed and cut into
  1-inch pieces

8 ounces green beans,
  trimmed and cut into
  1-inch pieces

2 orange sweet peppers,
  cored, seeded, and cut
  into ¼-inch strips

1 pound spaghetti

¾ cup half-and-half

¾ cup chicken broth

¾ teaspoon salt

¼ teaspoon ground black
  pepper

¼ teaspoon ground nutmeg

2 tablespoons olive oil

5 cloves garlic, sliced

2 cups grape tomatoes,
  halved

⅓ cup grated Parmesan
  cheese

¼ cup fresh flat-leaf parsley,
  chopped

  Shaved Parmesan cheese
  (optional)

1 Bring a large pot of salted water to a boil. Add asparagus and green beans; cook for 4 minutes. Add peppers and cook 1 more minute. Scoop out vegetables with a large slotted spoon and place in a colander. Rinse under cold water.

2 Add pasta to boiling water and cook according to package directions. Drain; return to pot.

3 While pasta is cooking, place half-and-half, chicken broth, salt, pepper, and nutmeg in a small saucepan. Bring to a simmer over medium heat.

4 Heat a large nonstick skillet over medium-high heat. Add olive oil and garlic and cook for 30 seconds. Add cooked vegetables and tomatoes. Cook, stirring a few times, for about 1½ minutes. Spoon into pasta pot. Stir grated cheese into the half-and-half mixture. Add to pasta and gently stir in parsley until all ingredients are combined. Allow to stand for 5 minutes. Shave Parmesan on top, if desired.

Nutrition facts per serving: 425 cal., 11 g total fat (5 g sat. fat), 18 mg chol., 447 mg sodium, 67 g carb., 17 g protein.

rigatoni ALLA SICILIANA

Prep: 10 minutes
Cook: 22 minutes
Makes: 6 servings

1 **eggplant (about
    1½ pounds)**

3 **cloves garlic, sliced**

3 **tablespoons olive oil**

1 **28-ounce can fire-roasted
    whole tomatoes**

1½ **teaspoons dried oregano**

1½ **teaspoons salt**

¼ **teaspoon crushed red
    pepper**

1 **pound mini rigatoni**

1 **cup shredded smoked
    mozzarella cheese
    (4 ounces)**

1 Trim eggplant and cut into ½-inch pieces. In a large skillet, cook eggplant and garlic in hot oil for 7 minutes over medium-high heat, stirring occasionally.

2 Stir in tomatoes and break up with a wooden spoon. Add oregano, salt, and crushed red pepper. Simmer for 15 minutes, stirring occasionally.

3 While sauce is simmering, cook pasta according to package directions. Drain and reserve 1 cup of the cooking water.

4 Toss drained pasta with sauce. Add reserved pasta water, in ¼-cup increments, until desired consistency.

5 Stir in cheese and allow to melt slightly; serve.

Nutrition facts per serving: 451 cal., 13 g total fat (3 g sat. fat), 15 mg chol., 996 mg sodium, 68 g carb., 16 g protein.

ravioli WITH MUSHROOM-WINE SAUCE

Elegant and superbly flavored, this dish is sure to impress company. Round out the menu with asparagus or sugar snap peas, a tossed salad, and French bread.

Prep: 20 minutes
Cook: 4 to 6 hours (low)
     or 2 to 3 hours
     (high)
Makes: 4 servings

- **4 cups sliced fresh button mushrooms**
- **4 cups sliced fresh portobello, shiitake, and/or cremini mushrooms**
- **2 14.5-ounce cans diced tomatoes**
- **½ cup water**
- **⅓ cup dry red wine**
- **4 cloves garlic, minced**
- **½ teaspoon salt**
- **¼ teaspoon dried rosemary, crushed**
- **¼ teaspoon crushed red pepper**
- **1 9-ounce package fresh cheese-filled ravioli**
- **Shredded Parmesan cheese**

1 In a 4- to 5-quart slow cooker, combine mushrooms, undrained tomatoes, water, red wine, garlic, salt, rosemary, and crushed red pepper.

2 Cover; cook on low-heat setting for 4 to 6 hours or on high-heat setting for 2 to 3 hours.

3 If using low-heat setting, turn slow cooker to high-heat setting. Stir ravioli into soup. Cover; cook for 20 minutes more. Serve with Parmesan cheese.

Nutrition facts per serving: 360 cal., 7 g total fat (3 g sat. fat), 32 mg chol., 1068 mg sodium, 62 g carb., 18 g protein.

meat, POULTRY, AND FISH

**Italian Braised Chicken with
Fennel and Cannellini,** *page 212*

chianti-braised STUFFED MEAT LOAF

Prep: 40 minutes
Bake: 55 minutes
Stand: 10 minutes
Oven: 350°F
Makes: 8 servings

2 eggs, lightly beaten

⅔ cup shredded Parmesan cheese

½ cup seasoned fine dry bread crumbs

½ cup thinly sliced scallions (4)

½ cup snipped fresh basil

¼ cup tomato paste

¼ cup Chianti or other dry red wine

2 cloves garlic, minced

¼ teaspoon salt

2 pounds ground beef sirloin*

Cheese Filling**

½ cup Chianti or other dry red wine

2 tablespoons Chianti or other dry red wine

½ cup sliced fresh mozzarella cheese (2 ounces)

Fresh Italian (flat-leaf) parsley sprigs and/or small basil leaves

1 Preheat oven to 350°F. In a large bowl, combine eggs, Parmesan cheese, bread crumbs, green onions, basil, tomato paste, ¼ cup wine, garlic, and salt. Add ground beef; mix well. Divide meat mixture in half.

2 In a 3-quart rectangular baking dish, pat half of the meat mixture into a 9x5-inch rectangle, building up the edges to make a 1-inch-deep well in the center. Spoon Cheese Filling into the well. Top with the remaining meat mixture; pinch top and bottom edges together to seal. If necessary, gently reshape loaf into a 9x5-inch rectangle. Pour ½ cup wine into dish around loaf.

3 Bake for 50 to 60 minutes or until an instant-read thermometer inserted in the meat registers 160°F. Spoon 2 tablespoons wine over meat loaf; top with mozzarella cheese. Bake about 5 minutes more or until cheese is melted.

4 Let stand for 10 minutes before serving. Using two large spatulas, transfer meat loaf to a serving platter. Garnish with parsley and/or basil.

Cheese Filling: In a medium bowl, combine 1 cup shredded mozzarella or provolone cheese (4 ounces), ½ cup chopped toasted pine nuts, ½ cup finely chopped oil-pack dried tomatoes, 3 tablespoons snipped fresh basil, 1 tablespoon oil from jar of dried tomatoes, and, if desired, ½ teaspoon finely shredded lemon peel.

Nutrition facts per serving: 474 cal., 30 g total fat (11 g sat. fat), 123 mg chol., 566 mg sodium, 12 g carb., 35 g protein.

*Tip: If desired, use a mixture of ground beef, bulk mild Italian sausage, and ground turkey.

eggplant AND BEEF CASSEROLE

Eggplant, ground beef, sweet pepper, and Italian blend cheese join forces in this delicious dinner-in-a-dish.

Prep: 50 minutes
Bake: 30 minutes
Stand: 10 minutes
Oven: 350°F
Makes: 8 servings

¾ **cup milk**

1 **egg, beaten**

¾ **cup all-purpose flour**

½ **teaspoon salt**

¼ **teaspoon ground black pepper**

1 **1½-pound eggplant, peeled and cut into ½-inch-thick slices**

3 **tablespoons vegetable oil**

1 **pound lean ground beef**

1 **large green sweet pepper, chopped (1 cup)**

1 **medium onion, chopped (¾ cup)**

1 **15-ounce can tomato sauce**

1 **8-ounce can tomato sauce**

1½ **teaspoons dried Italian seasoning, crushed**

2 **cups shredded Italian blend cheese (8 ounces)**

1 Grease a 3-quart rectangular baking dish; set aside. In a small bowl, combine milk and egg. In a shallow dish combine flour, salt, and pepper.

2 Dip eggplant slices into egg mixture; coat with flour mixture. In a 12-inch skillet, heat oil over medium heat. Add several of the eggplant slices; cook for about 4 minutes or until golden brown, turning once. Repeat with remaining eggplant slices, adding more oil if necessary. Drain on paper towels.

3 Preheat oven to 350°F. In a large skillet, cook ground beef, sweet pepper, and onion until meat is cooked through, using a wooden spoon to break up meat as it cooks; drain off fat. Stir tomato sauce and Italian seasoning into meat mixture.

4 Layer half of the eggplant slices in the prepared baking dish, cutting slices to fit. Spread with half of the meat mixture; sprinkle with half of the cheese. Repeat layers. Cover dish with foil.

5 Bake for 20 minutes. Uncover and bake for 10 to 15 minutes more or until heated through. Let stand for 10 minutes before serving.

Nutrition facts per serving: 340 cal., 19 g total fat (7 g sat. fat), 84 mg chol., 796 mg sodium, 23 g carb., 22 g protein.

individual SICILIAN MEAT LOAVES

Start to Finish: 30 minutes
Oven: 400°F
Makes: 4 servings

1 egg, lightly beaten

1¾ cups bottled garlic and
    onion pasta sauce

¼ cup seasoned fine dry
    bread crumbs

¼ teaspoon salt

¼ teaspoon ground
    black pepper

12 ounces lean ground beef

2 ounces mozzarella cheese

4 thin slices prosciutto
    or cooked ham (about
    2 ounces)

1 9-ounce package fresh
    plain or spinach
    fettuccine

    Finely shredded Parmesan
    cheese (optional)

1 Preheat oven to 400°F. In a medium bowl, combine egg, ¼ cup of the pasta sauce, bread crumbs, salt, and pepper. Add ground beef; mix well.

2 Cut mozzarella cheese into four logs measuring approximately 2¼x¾x½ inches. Wrap a slice of prosciutto around each cheese log. Shape one-fourth of the ground beef mixture around each cheese log to form a loaf. Flatten the meat loaves to 1½ inches thick and place in a shallow baking pan.

3 Bake loaves, uncovered, for about 20 minutes or until internal temperature of the beef registers 160°F on an instant-read thermometer.

4 Meanwhile, cook pasta according to package directions. Heat remaining pasta sauce in a small saucepan over medium heat until bubbly.

5 To serve, arrange meat loaves on hot cooked pasta. Spoon sauce over top. If desired, sprinkle with Parmesan cheese.

Nutrition facts per serving: 631 cal., 31 g total fat (12 g sat. fat), 173 mg chol., 1132 mg sodium, 55 g carb., 31 g protein.

easy ITALIAN PEPPER STEAK

Bring an Italian restaurant favorite home in a hurry. Frozen pepper stir-fry vegetables and spiced Italian tomato sauce serve as the shortcuts.

Start to Finish: 25 minutes
Makes: 4 servings

- 1 9-ounce package fresh fettuccine
- 12 ounces boneless beef top sirloin steak, cut into thin, bite-size strips
- ¼ teaspoon crushed red pepper
- 2 tablespoons olive oil
- 1 pound package frozen pepper stir-fry vegetables (yellow, green and red sweet peppers and onion), thawed and well drained
- 2 tablespoons balsamic vinegar
- 1 15-ounce can chunky Italian-style tomato sauce
- 2 tablespoons toasted pine nuts (optional)
  Crushed red pepper (optional)

1 Cook pasta according to package directions. Drain and keep warm.

2 Meanwhile, combine steak strips and ¼ teaspoon crushed red pepper; set aside.

3 Heat 1 tablespoon of the oil in a large skillet; add thawed pepper blend. Stir-fry for 2 to 3 minutes or till crisp-tender. Carefully add balsamic vinegar; toss to coat. Remove from skillet. Cover and keep warm.

4 Heat remaining oil in the same skillet; add beef. Stir-fry for 2 to 3 minutes or till tender. Add tomato sauce; heat through.

5 Toss beef mixture with pasta and vegetables. If desired, sprinkle with pine nuts and pass additional crushed red pepper at the table.

Nutrition facts per serving: 415 cal., 11 g total fat (2 g sat. fat), 87 mg chol., 648 mg sodium, 50 g carb., 28 g protein.

italian STEAK ROLLS

Stuffed with veggies and Parmesan cheese, these beef bundles cook up moist and tender in bottled meatless spaghetti sauce.

Prep: 35 minutes
Cook: 8 to 10 hours (low)
or 4 to 5 hours
(high)
Makes: 6 servings

½ **cup shredded carrot**

⅓ **cup chopped zucchini**

⅓ **cup chopped red or green sweet pepper**

¼ **cup sliced scallions**

2 **tablespoons grated Parmesan cheese**

1 **tablespoon snipped fresh parsley**

1 **clove garlic, minced**

¼ **teaspoon ground black pepper**

6 **tenderized beef round steaks (about 2 pounds total)***

2 **cups marinara sauce**

1 For the vegetable filling, in a small bowl, combine carrot, zucchini, sweet pepper, scallions, Parmesan cheese, parsley, garlic, and black pepper. Spoon ¼ cup of the vegetable filling onto each piece of meat. Roll up meat around the filling; secure with 100% cotton kitchen string or wooden toothpicks.

2 Place meat rolls in a 3½- or 4-quart slow cooker. Pour marinara sauce over the meat rolls.

3 Cover; cook on low-heat setting for 8 to 10 hours or on high-heat setting for 4 to 5 hours. Discard string or toothpicks. Serve sauce with meat rolls.

Nutrition facts per serving: 261 cal., 9 g total fat (3 g sat. fat), 73 mg chol., 523 mg sodium, 7 g carb., 36 g protein.

***Test Kitchen Tip:** If you can't find tenderized round steak, ask a butcher to tenderize 2 pounds boneless beef round steak and cut it into six pieces. Or cut 2 pounds boneless beef round steak into six serving-size pieces; place each steak piece between two pieces of plastic wrap. Using a meat mallet, pound the steak pieces until ¼ to ½ inch thick.

italian BEEF SKILLET

Prep: 30 minutes
Cook: 1 hour 15 minutes
Makes: 6 servings

1 pound boneless beef round steak

2 cups sliced fresh mushrooms

2 medium onions, chopped

1 medium green sweet pepper, seeded and chopped

1 stalk celery, chopped

1 14.5-ounce can diced tomatoes with garlic, basil, and oregano, undrained

2 tablespoons water

⅛ to ¼ teaspoon crushed red pepper

6 ounces dried whole wheat or multigrain pasta, cooked and kept warm

Snipped fresh parsley (optional)

2 tablespoons grated Parmesan cheese

1 Trim fat from meat. Cut meat into six serving-size pieces. Lightly coat an unheated large nonstick skillet with nonstick cooking spray. Preheat over medium heat. Add meat and cook until brown, turning to brown evenly. Remove meat from skillet; set aside.

2 Add mushrooms, onions, sweet pepper, and celery to skillet. Cook for about 5 minutes or until vegetables are nearly tender, stirring occasionally. Stir in tomatoes, the water, and crushed red pepper. Return meat to skillet, spooning vegetable mixture over meat. Bring to boiling; reduce heat. Cover and simmer for about 1¼ hours or until meat is tender, stirring occasionally.

3 Place steak on hot cooked pasta. Spoon vegetable mixture over steak. If desired, sprinkle with parsley. Serve with Parmesan cheese.

Nutrition facts per serving: 269 cal., 5 g total fat (2 g sat. fat), 51 mg chol., 431 mg sodium, 32 g carb., 24 g protein.

fontina-stuffed
TENDERLOIN STEAKS

Prep: 25 minutes
Roast: 12 minutes
Oven: 400°F
Makes: 2 servings

2 6-ounce beef tenderloin
    steaks

½ cup shredded Fontina
    cheese (2 ounces)

1 tablespoon finely
    chopped oil-pack dried
    tomatoes

1 teaspoon snipped fresh
    Italian (flat-leaf) parsley

½ teaspoon fresh thyme
    leaves

1 small clove garlic, minced

1 thin slice prosciutto,
    halved

    Salt and ground
    black pepper

1 tablespoon olive oil

    Snipped fresh Italian
    (flat-leaf) parsley
    (optional)

1 Preheat oven to 400°F. Trim fat from steaks. Make a pocket in each steak by cutting horizontally from one side almost to the opposite side. Set aside.

2 For filling, in a small bowl, combine cheese, dried tomatoes, 1 teaspoon parsley, thyme, and garlic. Divide filling between prosciutto halves; loosely roll up prosciutto around filling. Insert prosciutto bundles into pockets in steaks; secure with wooden toothpicks. Sprinkle steaks with salt and pepper.

3 In a medium skillet, cook steaks in hot oil over medium-high heat until brown on both sides. Place steaks on a rack in a shallow baking pan. Roast for 12 to 15 minutes for medium-rare (145°F) to medium (160°F). Remove and discard toothpicks. If desired, sprinkle steaks with additional parsley.

Nutrition facts per serving: 623 cal., 49 g total fat (19 g sat. fat), 145 mg chol., 688 mg sodium, 2 g carb., 43 g protein.

beef PEPPER AND PESTO KABOBS

Brushing on pesto adds major flavor to these tender sirloin skewers.

Prep: 25 minutes
Start to Finish: 35 minutes
Makes: 6 servings

1¾ **pounds boneless beef sirloin steak, cut into 1-inch cubes**

2 **large red sweet peppers, seeded and cut into 1-inch pieces**

3 **tablespoons olive oil**

1 **teaspoon salt**

8 **ounces linguine or fettuccine**

⅓ **cup prepared pesto**

⅔ **cup finely grated Parmesan cheese**

½ **teaspoon ground black pepper**

1 Thread meat and peppers onto skewers and brush with 2 tablespoons oil. Season with salt.

2 Cook pasta according to package directions. Meanwhile, heat grill to medium high; oil grill grates and cook kabobs, turning frequently, until the meat is done, 7 to 9 minutes for medium. Remove from grill. Using a clean brush or spoon, coat meat generously with pesto.

3 Toss drained pasta with Parmesan, remaining 1 tablespoon oil, and black pepper; serve with kabobs.

Nutrition facts per serving: 485 cal., 21 g total fat (5.5 g sat. fat), 66 mg chol., 622 mg sodium, 33 g carb., 39 g protein.

lamb WITH EGGPLANT RELISH

Prep: 20 minutes
Cook: 12 minutes
Grill: 12 minutes
Makes: 4 servings

½ cup extra virgin olive oil

1 large red onion, chopped (2 cups)

6 cloves garlic, minced

1 large eggplant, cut in ¾-inch cubes (about 1¼ pounds; 6 cups)

½ teaspoon salt

¼ teaspoon ground black pepper

1 14-ounce can whole peeled plum tomatoes in puree

2 or 3 medium oranges

1 tablespoon sugar

8 lamb loin chops, about 1 inch thick (about 1½ pounds)

8 slices baguette, toasted

8 fresh thyme sprigs

1 In a very large skillet, heat ⅓ cup oil over medium-high heat. Add onion and 4 cloves garlic; cook for 1 minute. Add eggplant, salt, and pepper. Cook and stir for 8 minutes or until eggplant is tender. Add undrained tomatoes, crushing with a spoon. Cook for 4 minutes or until most liquid is gone, stirring occasionally.

2 Meanwhile, finely shred enough orange peel to make 2 teaspoons. Peel and section two oranges over a bowl to catch juices. If necessary, squeeze juice from remaining orange to make 3 tablespoons. Stir orange sections, orange peel, orange juice, and sugar into eggplant relish.

3 In a small bowl, stir together remaining oil and garlic. Brush lamb with oil mixture; season with salt and pepper. For gas grill, preheat grill. Reduce heat to medium. Place chops on grill rack over heat. Grill for 12 to 14 minutes for medium-rare (145°F), turning chops once halfway through grilling.

4 Drizzle relish with additional olive oil. Divide relish among eight plates. Add a lamb chop, baguette slice, and thyme sprig to each.

Nutrition facts per serving: 626 cal., 41 g total fat (7 g sat. fat), 90 mg chol., 735 mg sodium, 33 g carb., 33 g protein.

tuscan LAMB SKILLET

Forget the mint jelly for these chops. A toss of white beans, tomatoes, olive oil, garlic, and rosemary brings a taste of Italy to your table.

Start to Finish: 20 minutes
Makes: 4 servings

8   lamb rib chops, cut 1 inch thick (1½ pounds)

2   teaspoons olive oil

3   cloves garlic, minced

1   19-ounce can white kidney beans, rinsed and drained

1   8-ounce can Italian-style stewed tomatoes

1   tablespoon balsamic vinegar

2   teaspoons snipped fresh rosemary

    Fresh rosemary (optional)

1 Trim fat from lamb chops. In a large skillet, cook chops in hot oil over medium heat for about 8 minutes or until a thermometer inserted in center registers 160°F for medium doneness, turning once. Transfer chops to a large plate; keep warm.

2 Stir garlic into drippings in skillet. Cook and stir for 1 minute. Stir in beans, undrained tomatoes, vinegar, and rosemary. Bring to boiling; reduce heat. Simmer, uncovered, for 3 minutes.

3 Spoon bean mixture onto four dinner plates; arrange two chops on each plate. If desired, garnish with additional rosemary.

Nutrition facts per serving: 272 cal., 9 g total fat (3 g sat. fat), 67 mg chol., 466 mg sodium, 24 g carb., 30 g protein.

herb-scented TUSCAN PORK LOIN

Prep: 20 minutes
Chill: 8 to 24 hours
Roast: 2 hours
Stand: 15 minutes
Oven: 325°F
Makes: 12 to 15 servings

3 tablespoons snipped
  fresh rosemary

8 cloves garlic, minced

4 teaspoons finely
  shredded lemon peel

1 teaspoon salt

1 4½- to 5-pound boneless
  pork top loin roast
  (double loin, tied)

4 ounces thinly sliced
  pancetta

1 In a small bowl, combine rosemary, garlic, lemon peel, and salt.

2 Untie meat; trim fat from meat. Spread rosemary mixture over top of one of the loins. Place pancetta on top of the other loin. Reassemble meat, placing the pancetta-topped loin on top and positioning the rosemary mixture in the middle. Retie with 100% cotton kitchen string. Wrap meat tightly in plastic wrap and chill for 8 to 24 hours.

3 Preheat oven to 325°F. Place meat on a rack in a shallow roasting pan. Insert a meat thermometer into center of meat. Roast for 2 to 2½ hours or until meat thermometer registers 150°F.

4 Cover meat with foil and let stand for 15 minutes. The temperature of the meat after standing should be 160°F. Slice meat and serve.

Nutrition facts per serving: 286 cal., 12 g total fat (4 g sat. fat), 99 mg chol., 396 mg sodium, 1 g carb., 39 g protein.

pork CHOPS WITH HERB-TOMATO SAUCE

Set the slow cooker to low and let the meat soak in the tomato sauce's zesty herbs and spices.

Prep: 20 minutes
Cook: 7 to 8 hours (low) or
       3½ to 4 hours (high)
Makes: 4 servings

- 4 pork rib chops (with bone), cut ¾ inch thick (about 1¾ pounds)
- 1 small onion, chopped
- 2 teaspoons quick-cooking tapioca, crushed*
- 1½ teaspoons bottled minced garlic (3 cloves)
- 1 teaspoon dried Italian seasoning, crushed
- ½ teaspoon ground black pepper
- ½ teaspoon Worcestershire sauce
- ¼ teaspoon salt
- ¼ teaspoon crushed red pepper
- 2 14.5-ounce cans no-salt-added stewed tomatoes, undrained

1 Trim fat from chops. Coat 12-inch skillet with cooking spray; heat over medium-high heat. Brown chops on both sides in hot skillet.

2 In a 3½- or 4-quart slow cooker, combine onion, tapioca, garlic, Italian seasoning, black pepper, Worcestershire sauce, salt, and crushed red pepper. Add chops. Pour tomatoes over chops.

3 Cover and cook on low-heat setting for 7 to 8 hours or on high-heat setting for 3½ to 4 hours.

4 To serve, transfer chops to serving platter. Spoon tomatoes atop chops using a slotted spoon. If desired, pour some of the cooking liquid atop chops and tomatoes.

Nutrition facts per serving: 241 cal., 6 g total fat (2 g sat. fat), 62 mg chol., 287 mg sodium, 19 g carb., 27 g protein.

*Tip: Crush tapioca with a mortar and pestle or in a spice grinder.

veal PICCATA

Start to Finish: 25 minutes
Makes: 4 servings

1 **lemon**

6 **ounces whole wheat orzo
(about 1 cup)**

1 **cup cherry tomatoes,
halved**

¼ **cup capers, rinsed and
drained**

2 **teaspoons snipped fresh
rosemary, or ½ teaspoon
dried rosemary, crushed**

1 **tablespoon olive oil**

1 **pound veal scaloppine
(about ¼ inch thick)**

¼ **teaspoon salt**

¼ **teaspoon ground black
pepper**

¼ **cup dry white wine**

1 **tablespoon snipped fresh
flat-leaf parsley**

**Fresh rosemary sprigs
(optional)**

Lemon wedges (optional)

1 Finely shred the peel from the lemon. Squeeze the juice from the lemon. Cook orzo in lightly salted boiling water according to package directions; drain. Stir in half of the lemon peel, half of the lemon juice, the cherry tomatoes, half of the capers, and the snipped or dried rosemary. Cover and let stand until serving time.

2 Meanwhile, in a very large skillet, heat oil over medium-high heat. Sprinkle veal with salt and pepper. Add veal to skillet. Cook for about 4 minutes or until no longer pink, turning veal occasionally to brown evenly. Transfer veal to a serving platter; cover and keep warm.

3 Add the remaining lemon peel, remaining lemon juice, remaining capers, and the white wine to the skillet. Bring to boiling, scraping the browned bits from the bottom of the pan.

4 Pour wine mixture over veal. Serve with cooked orzo. Sprinkle orzo mixture with parsley. If desired, garnish with rosemary sprigs and serve with lemon wedges.

Nutrition facts per serving: 329 cal., 7 g total fat (1 g sat. fat), 89 mg chol., 481 mg sodium, 35 g carb., 30 g protein.

veal SALTIMBOCCA

It only takes one bite of these delicious veal rolls, filled with prosciutto and fresh sage, then simmered in a white wine sauce, to know why saltimbocca translates as "jump in your mouth."

Prep: 20 minutes
Cook: 5 minutes
Makes: 4 servings

12 ounces boneless veal leg top round steak or veal leg sirloin steak, cut ¼ inch thick, or 12 ounces boneless, skinless chicken breast halves

4 slices prosciutto (2 ounces), halved, or 2 thin slices cooked ham, quartered

8 fresh sage leaves

2 teaspoons olive oil or cooking oil

Ground black pepper

⅓ cup dry white wine

2 tablespoons snipped fresh parsley

2 tablespoons grated Parmesan cheese

2 cups hot cooked rice

1 Rinse chicken (if using); pat dry with paper towels. Cut veal or chicken into 8 pieces. Place each piece of meat between two pieces of plastic wrap. Working from the center to the edges, pound the meat lightly with the flat side of a meat mallet to ⅛-inch thickness. Remove plastic wrap. Place a slice of prosciutto or ham on top of each piece of meat. Add a sage leaf; secure with a wooden toothpick.

2 Heat the oil in a 12-inch skillet over medium-high heat for 1 minute. Add the veal or chicken. Cook for 1 to 2 minutes on each side or until tender and no longer pink. Season with the pepper. Remove meat from skillet; cover and keep warm.

3 Remove skillet from heat; let cool for 1 minute. Carefully add wine. Return skillet to heat; cook for 2 to 3 minutes or until wine is reduced slightly, scraping up browned bits in skillet. Add pan juices, parsley, and Parmesan cheese to the rice; toss to combine. Remove toothpicks from meat. Serve meat on top of rice.

Nutrition facts per serving: 333 cal., 11 g total fat (2 g sat. fat), 71 mg chol., 388 mg sodium, 27 g carb., 27 g protein.

chicken SCALOPPINE ALLA MARSALA

Prep: 15 minutes
Cook: 27 minutes
Makes: 6 servings

- ¼ **cup rice flour**
- 6 **thin-cut skinless, boneless chicken breasts, about 4 ounces each**
- 3 **tablespoons olive oil**
- 1 **8-ounce package sliced brown mushrooms**
- ½ **cup Marsala wine**
- ½ **cup low-sodium beef broth**
- ¼ **teaspoon salt**
- ⅛ **teaspoon ground black pepper**
- 1 **10-ounce package brown rice couscous**
- 1 **tablespoon unsalted butter**
- 1 **tablespoon chopped fresh parsley**

1 Place the rice flour on a large plate. Coat the chicken with the flour. Heat a large nonstick skillet over medium-high heat. Add 1 tablespoon of oil and sauté half the chicken for 1 to 2 minutes per side, until lightly browned. Remove to a plate and keep warm. Repeat with a second tablespoon of the oil and the remaining chicken.

2 Add the remaining tablespoon oil to the skillet and stir in the mushrooms. Cook for 2 to 3 minutes, until tender. Off heat, add the Marsala and cook for 1 minute, scraping any browned bits from the skillet. Add the broth, salt, and pepper. Bring to a simmer and return the chicken and any accumulated juices to skillet. Gently simmer, covered, for 15 minutes.

3 Meanwhile, prepare couscous following package directions.

4 Stir butter and parsley into sauce and serve with cooked couscous.

Nutrition facts per serving: 429 cal., 14 g total fat (3 g sat. fat), 78 mg chol., 410 mg sodium, 43 g carb., 32 g protein.

chicken WITH CREAMY CHIVE SAUCE

Italian salad dressing mix, golden mushroom soup, wine, and cream cheese with chives and onion add up to an incredible sauce for chicken. If you can afford the extra carbohydrates, serve the chicken and sauce over hot cooked pasta.

Prep: 15 minutes
Cook: 4 to 5 hours (low)
Makes: 6 servings

6 **skinless, boneless chicken breast halves (about 1½ pounds total)**

¼ **cup butter**

1 **0.7-ounce package Italian salad dressing mix**

1 **10.75-ounce can condensed golden mushroom soup**

½ **cup dry white wine**

½ **of an 8-ounce tub cream cheese with chives and onion**

Snipped fresh chives (optional)

1 Place chicken in a 3½- or 4-quart slow cooker. In a medium saucepan, melt the butter. Stir in Italian salad dressing mix. Add golden mushroom soup, wine, and cream cheese, stirring until combined. Pour over the chicken.

2 Cover; cook on low-heat setting for 4 to 5 hours. Serve chicken with sauce. If desired, sprinkle with fresh chives.

Nutrition facts per serving: 310 cal., 17 g total fat (9 g sat. fat), 110 mg chol., 1043 mg sodium, 6 g carb., 28 g protein.

saucy CHICKEN PARMESAN

Prep: 20 minutes
Bake: 15 minutes
Oven: 400°F
Makes: 4 servings

4 skinless, boneless
   chicken breast halves
   (1 to 1½ pounds)

1 egg white, lightly beaten

1 tablespoon water

¾ cup cornflakes, crushed
   (about ⅓ cup)

2 tablespoons grated
   Parmesan cheese

¼ teaspoon dried Italian
   seasoning, basil, or
   oregano, crushed,
   or 1 teaspoon snipped
   fresh basil or oregano

⅛ teaspoon ground
   black pepper

1⅓ cups spaghetti sauce

4 ounces spaghetti,
   fettuccine, or other
   pasta, cooked according
   to package directions
   and drained

   Grated Parmesan cheese
   (optional)

   Fresh herb sprigs
   (optional)

❶ Preheat oven to 400°F. Place each piece of chicken between 2 pieces of plastic wrap. Using the flat side of a meat mallet, lightly pound to flatten slightly (about ½ inch thick). Remove plastic wrap.

❷ Lightly coat a shallow baking pan with nonstick cooking spray. In a shallow dish, combine egg white and the water. In another shallow dish, combine crushed cornflakes, the 2 tablespoons Parmesan cheese, the Italian seasoning, and pepper. Dip chicken pieces, one at a time, into egg mixture; coat with crumb mixture. Place coated chicken pieces in prepared baking pan.

❸ Bake for about 15 minutes or until chicken is tender and no longer pink (170°F).

❹ Meanwhile, in a small saucepan warm spaghetti sauce over low heat. Divide pasta among four dinner plates. Place chicken on top of pasta. Spoon spaghetti sauce over chicken. If desired, sprinkle with additional Parmesan cheese and garnish with fresh herb sprigs.

Nutrition facts per serving: 312 cal., 3 g total fat (1 g sat. fat), 68 mg chol., 566 mg sodium, 37 g carb., 34 g protein.

chicken TENDERS PARMESAN

Start to Finish: 20 minutes
Oven: 425°F
Makes: 4 servings

- 1 **12-ounce package frozen, cooked, breaded chicken breast tenders**
- 1 **cup bottled marinara sauce**
- ½ **cup shredded Italian blend cheese**
- 2 **tablespoons snipped fresh basil (optional)**

Preheat oven to 425°F. Place chicken tenders in a 2-quart square baking dish. Top with marinara sauce and cheese. Bake for 15 minutes or until hot and bubbly. If desired, sprinkle with fresh basil.

Nutrition facts per serving: 279 cal., 14 g total fat (4 g sat. fat), 35 mg chol., 863 mg sodium, 23 g carb., 17 g protein.

chicken SPIEDINI

Prep: 30 minutes
Marinate: 2 hours
Grill: 10 minutes
Cook: 5 minutes
Makes: 4 servings

1¼ pounds chicken breast tenderloins

⅔ cup bottled sweet Italian or Italian dressing

¾ cup seasoned fine dry bread crumbs

¾ cup halved fresh mushrooms

2 cloves garlic, minced

1 tablespoon butter

¼ cup coarsely chopped prosciutto

¾ cup shredded provel or mozzarella cheese (3 ounces)

1 lemon, quartered

1 Place chicken in a resealable plastic bag set in a shallow dish. Pour salad dressing over chicken. Seal bag; turn to coat chicken. Marinate in the refrigerator for 2 to 24 hours, turning bag occasionally.

2 Drain chicken, discarding dressing. Place bread crumbs in a shallow dish. Dip chicken in bread crumbs to coat. On five or six long metal skewers, thread chicken, accordion-style, leaving ¼-inch space between each piece.

3 For a charcoal grill, grill skewers on the rack of an uncovered grill directly over medium coals for 10 to 12 minutes or until chicken is tender and no longer pink (170°F), turning once halfway through grilling. (For a gas grill, preheat grill. Reduce heat to medium. Place skewers on grill rack over heat. Cover and grill as directed.)

4 Meanwhile, in a large skillet, cook mushrooms and garlic in hot butter over medium heat for about 5 minutes or until mushrooms are just tender, stirring occasionally. Add prosciutto; cook and stir for 2 minutes more.

5 Remove chicken from skewers; arrange on a serving plate. Sprinkle the chicken with half of the cheese. Spoon mushroom mixture over chicken. Sprinkle with the remaining cheese. Squeeze a lemon wedge over each serving.

Nutrition facts per serving: 471 cal., 22 g total fat (6 g sat. fat), 113 mg chol., 1820 mg sodium, 22 g carb., 46 g protein.

Oven Directions: Arrange skewers in a 15x10x1-inch baking pan. Bake for about 15 minutes or until chicken is no longer pink (170°F).

baked CHICKEN CACCIATORE

Cacciatore means "hunter" in Italian. Some say this dish was devised by clever cooks when hunters came home from the hunt empty-handed.

Prep: 20 minutes
Bake: 30 minutes
Oven: 375°F
Makes: 4 servings

- 8 **skinless, boneless chicken thighs (about 2 pounds total)**
- 1 **tablespoon olive oil**
- 1 **teaspoon dried oregano, crushed**
- ¼ **teaspoon ground black pepper**
- 3 **cups sliced fresh mushrooms**
- 1 **large green sweet pepper, cut into ½-inch-wide strips**
- 1 **medium onion, chopped**
- 1 **10.75-ounce can condensed tomato soup**
- 1 **tablespoon snipped fresh parsley**

  Hot cooked mashed potatoes (optional)

1 Preheat oven to 375°F. In a very large ovenproof skillet, brown chicken in hot oil, turning to brown evenly. Drain off fat. Sprinkle browned chicken with oregano and black pepper. Add mushrooms, sweet pepper, and onion to skillet. Cover and bake for 20 minutes.

2 Stir in tomato soup. Bake, uncovered, for about 10 minutes more or until chicken is no longer pink (180°F) and vegetables are crisp-tender. Sprinkle with parsley. If desired, serve with mashed potatoes.

Nutrition facts per serving: 285 cal., 10 g total fat (2 g sat. fat), 115 mg chol., 587 mg sodium, 18 g carb., 31 g protein.

roasted ITALIAN CHICKEN

Prep: 20 minutes
Roast: 1 hour 15 minutes
Stand: 10 minutes
Oven: 375°F
Makes: 6 servings

2 **tablespoons balsamic vinegar**

2 **tablespoons olive oil**

1 **tablespoon lemon juice**

2 **teaspoons dried oregano, crushed**

2 **teaspoons dried basil, crushed**

4 **cloves garlic, minced**

1 **teaspoon salt**

1 **teaspoon dried thyme, crushed**

¾ **teaspoon ground black pepper**

1 **3- to 3½-pound whole broiler-fryer chicken**

Lemon wedges (optional)

1 Preheat oven to 375°F. In a small bowl, combine vinegar, oil, lemon juice, oregano, basil, garlic, salt, thyme, and pepper. Divide herb mixture in half.

2 Rinse inside of chicken; pat dry with paper towels. On one side of the chicken, slip your fingers between the skin and breast meat, forming a pocket; repeat on other side of chicken. Divide one portion of the herb mixture between pockets.

3 Using 100% cotton kitchen string, tie drumsticks to tail. Twist wing tips under back. Place chicken, breast side up, on a rack in a shallow roasting pan. If desired, insert a meat thermometer into the center of an inside thigh muscle, making sure the tip does not touch bone.

4 Roast, uncovered, for 1 hour. Cut string between drumsticks. Brush chicken with the remaining herb mixture. Roast for 15 to 30 minutes more or until thermometer registers 180°F, drumsticks move easily in their sockets, and juices run clear.

5 Transfer chicken to a serving platter. Cover with foil; let stand for 10 minutes before carving. If desired, serve with lemon wedges.

Nutrition facts per serving: 376 cal., 27 g total fat (7 g sat. fat), 115 mg chol., 476 mg sodium, 3 g carb., 29 g protein.

Tip: In a pinch, substitute 2 tablespoons of Italian seasoning for the basil, oregano, and thyme.

italian FRIED CHICKEN

Prep: 15 minutes
Cook: 22 minutes
Makes: 8 pieces

½ **cup all-purpose flour**

½ **cup seasoned dry bread crumbs**

½ **cup grated Parmesan cheese**

1 **teaspoon garlic salt**

2 **eggs**

2 **tablespoons milk**

½ **teaspoon salt**

1 **broiler-fryer chicken (about 3½ pounds), cut into 8 pieces**

2 **cups peanut oil**

1 In a shallow dish, whisk together flour, bread crumbs, Parmesan and garlic salt. In a medium bowl, whisk together eggs, milk, and salt.

2 Dip each piece of chicken into the egg mixture, shaking off excess. Roll in flour mixture and place on a baking sheet fitted with wire rack. Refrigerate while heating oil.

3 Place oil in a large, lidded, heavy-bottom skillet. Heat oil to 365°F over medium-high heat. Add chicken, skin side down. Fry, covered, for about 22 minutes, turning every 4 minutes, or until internal temperature registers 170°F on an instant-read thermometer. Transfer chicken to paper towels.

Nutrition facts per serving: 410 cal., 32 g total fat (8 g sat. fat), 113 mg chol., 326 mg sodium, 6 g carb., 24 g protein.

italian CHICKEN AND VEGETABLES

Rely on this recipe when your schedule is jam-packed—just put three ingredients into the cooker and you can be on your way.

Prep: 15 minutes
Cook: 6 to 7 hours (low)
or 3 to 3½ hours
(high)
Makes: 4 servings

4 **small whole chicken legs (drumstick and thigh; 2½ to 3 pounds total), skin and fat removed**

1 **26-ounce jar roasted garlic pasta sauce**

1 **pound package frozen (yellow, green, and red) sweet peppers and onion stir-fry vegetables**

3 **cups hot cooked noodles**

⅓ **cup shredded mozzarella cheese or finely shredded Parmesan cheese**

1 Place chicken in a 3½- or 4-quart slow cooker. Add pasta sauce and frozen vegetables.

2 Cover and cook on low-heat setting for 6 to 7 hours or on high-heat setting for 3 to 3½ hours.

3 Serve the chicken and vegetable mixture with hot cooked noodles. Sprinkle with cheese.

Nutrition facts per serving: 500 cal., 12 g total fat (3 g sat. fat), 174 mg chol., 796 mg sodium, 52 g carb., 45 g protein.

italian BRAISED CHICKEN WITH FENNEL AND CANNELLINI

Prep: 30 minutes
Cook: 5 to 6 hours (low) or
2½ to 3 hours (high)
Makes: 6 servings

2 to 2½ pounds chicken drumsticks and/or thighs, skin removed

¾ teaspoon salt

¼ teaspoon ground black pepper

1 15-ounce can cannellini beans, rinsed and drained

1 bulb fennel, cored and cut into thin wedges

1 medium yellow sweet pepper, seeded and cut into 1-inch pieces

1 medium onion, cut into thin wedges

3 cloves garlic, minced

1 teaspoon snipped fresh rosemary

1 teaspoon snipped fresh oregano

¼ teaspoon crushed red pepper

1 14.5-ounce can diced tomatoes

½ cup dry white wine or reduced-sodium chicken broth

¼ cup tomato paste

¼ cup shaved Parmesan cheese

1 tablespoon snipped fresh Italian (flat-leaf) parsley

1 Sprinkle chicken pieces with ¼ teaspoon of the salt and the pepper. Place chicken in a 3½- to 4-quart slow cooker. Top with cannellini beans, fennel, sweet pepper, onion, garlic, rosemary, oregano, and crushed red pepper. In a medium bowl, combine tomatoes, white wine, tomato paste, and remaining ½ teaspoon salt; pour over mixture in cooker.

2 Cover; cook on low-heat setting for 5 to 6 hours or on high-heat setting for 2½ to 3 hours.

3 Sprinkle each serving with Parmesan cheese and parsley.

Nutrition facts per serving: 225 cal., 4 g total fat (1 g sat. fat), 68 mg chol., 777 mg sodium, 23 g carb., 25 g protein.

cheese-topped
MEAT LOAF

Prep: 15 minutes
Bake: 30 minutes
Oven: 350°F
Makes: 6 servings

1½ **pounds ground turkey**

½ **cup seasoned dry bread crumbs**

2 **eggs, lightly beaten**

1 **16-ounce jar marinara sauce**

2 **tablespoons dried onion flakes**

1½ **teaspoons dried oregano**

¾ **teaspoon salt**

½ **teaspoon ground black pepper**

1 **cup shredded Italian cheese blend**

   Cooked pasta (optional)

1 Preheat oven to 350°F. In a large bowl, mix ground turkey, bread crumbs, eggs, ½ cup marinara sauce, onion flakes, dried oregano, salt, and black pepper.

2 Form into an 8x4-inch loaf and bake in a greased baking dish for 30 minutes.

3 Spoon ½ cup marinara over the top and bake for an additional 30 minutes. Cover top of meat loaf with shredded Italian cheese blend and bake for 5 more minutes, until cheese is melted. Serve with cooked pasta tossed with remaining marinara sauce.

Nutrition facts per serving: 366 cal., 20 g total fat (7 g sat. fat), 174 mg chol., 1277 mg sodium, 16 g carb., 29 g protein.

turkey BREAST STUFFED WITH SAUSAGE, FENNEL, AND FIGS

Prep: 20 minutes
Grill: 1½ hours
Stand: 10 minutes
Makes: 10 to 12 servings

1 4- to 5-pound bone-in turkey breast

½ teaspoon salt

½ teaspoon ground black pepper

1 pound bulk or link sweet Italian sausage

12 scallions, thinly sliced

⅔ cup snipped dried figs

1½ teaspoons fennel seeds

2 tablespoons olive oil

¼ teaspoon salt

¼ teaspoon ground black pepper

1 Remove bone from turkey (you may want to ask the butcher to remove the bone for you). Place turkey, skin side down, between two pieces of plastic wrap. Working from the center to the edges, pound lightly with the flat side of a meat mallet to an even thickness. Remove plastic wrap. Sprinkle turkey with the ½ teaspoon salt and the ½ teaspoon pepper.

2 For stuffing, remove casings from sausage, if present. In a medium bowl, combine sausage, scallions, figs, and fennel seeds.

3 Spoon stuffing over half of the turkey; fold other half of turkey over stuffing. Tie in several places with 100% cotton kitchen string or secure with metal skewers. Rub skin with oil and sprinkle with the ¼ teaspoon salt and the ¼ teaspoon pepper.

4 For a charcoal grill, arrange medium-hot coals around a drip pan in a grill with a cover. Test for medium heat above pan. Place turkey on the grill rack over pan. Cover and grill for 1½ to 2 hours or until turkey is no longer pink (170°F) and center of stuffing registers 165°F. (For a gas grill, preheat grill. Reduce heat to medium. Adjust for indirect cooking. Cover and grill as above.)

5 Remove turkey from grill. Cover with foil and let stand for 10 minutes before carving.

Nutrition facts per serving: 364 cal., 18 g total fat (6 g sat. fat), 119 mg chol., 577 mg sodium, 8 g carb., 41 g protein.

tilapia PUTTANESCA

Start to Finish: 25 minutes
Makes: 4 servings

- **1 pound fresh or frozen skinless tilapia fillets**
- **⅛ teaspoon salt**
- **½ medium red onion, cut in wedges**
- **1 tablespoon olive oil**
- **2 cloves garlic, minced**
- **1 14.5-ounce can diced tomatoes**
- **2 teaspoons dried oregano, crushed**
- **¼ teaspoon crushed red pepper**
- **¼ cup pitted Kalamata olives**
- **1 tablespoon capers, drained (optional)**
- **2 tablespoons coarsely chopped fresh Italian (flat-leaf) parsley**

1 Thaw fish, if frozen. Rinse; pat dry with paper towels. Sprinkle with salt. Set aside.

2 In large skillet, cook onion in olive oil over medium heat for 8 minutes or until tender; stirring occasionally. Stir in garlic, undrained tomatoes, oregano, and crushed red pepper. Bring to boiling; reduce heat. Simmer, uncovered, for 5 minutes.

3 Add olives and capers to sauce. Top with tilapia fillets. Return sauce to boiling; reduce heat. Cook, covered, for 6 to 10 minutes or until fish flakes when tested with fork. Remove fish. Simmer sauce, uncovered, for 1 to 2 minutes more to thicken. To serve, spoon sauce over fish. Sprinkle with parsley.

Nutrition facts per serving: 182 cal., 6 g total fat (1 g sat. fat), 56 mg chol., 431 mg sodium, 8 g carb., 24 g protein.

tuna WITH TUSCAN BEANS

While Tuscans have been cooking with them for centuries, white beans are underrated in North America. White beans add a creamy richness to dishes quickly, simply, and healthfully.

Start to Finish: 20 minutes
Makes: 4 servings

- 1 **pound fresh or frozen tuna or swordfish steaks, cut 1 inch thick**
- ¼ **teaspoon salt**
- ¼ **teaspoon ground black pepper**
- 1 **tablespoon olive oil**
- 2 **cloves garlic, minced**
- 2 **teaspoons olive oil**
- 1 **14.5-ounce can Italian-style stewed tomatoes, undrained and cut up**
- 2 **teaspoons snipped fresh sage, or ¼ teaspoon ground sage**
- 1 **15-ounce can navy beans, rinsed and drained**
  Lemon wedges
  Fresh sage sprigs (optional)

1 Thaw fish, if frozen. Cut fish into four portions. Sprinkle both sides of fish with salt and pepper. Heat the 1 tablespoon oil in a large skillet over medium heat. Add the fish. Cook for 10 to 12 minutes or until fish flakes easily with a fork, turning once. (If using tuna, fish may still be pink in the center.)

2 Meanwhile, cook garlic in 2 teaspoons hot oil in a medium skillet for 15 seconds. Stir in tomatoes and snipped sage. Bring to boiling; reduce heat. Simmer, uncovered, for 5 minutes. Stir in beans; heat through.

3 To serve, remove the skin from fish, if present. Spoon some of the bean mixture onto four dinner plates. Place a fish portion on top of bean mixture on each plate. Serve with lemon wedges. If desired, garnish with sage sprigs.

Nutrition facts per serving: 339 cal., 8 g total fat (1 g sat. fat), 51 mg chol., 883 mg sodium, 30 g carb., 36 g protein.

cod WITH TOMATO-WINE SAUCE

You can substitute any mild, white-fleshed fish in this recipe. Look for flounder, haddock, or halibut.

Start to Finish: 30 minutes
Makes: 4 servings

1 **pound fresh or frozen skinless cod fillets**

1 **teaspoon dried oregano, crushed**

½ **teaspoon coarsely ground black pepper**

1 **tablespoon olive oil**

1⅓ **cups chopped roma tomatoes (4 medium)**

1 **small onion, cut into thin wedges**

¼ **cup sliced pitted black olives**

¼ **cup dry white wine or chicken broth**

1 **tablespoon capers, drained**

2 **cloves garlic, minced**

Fresh oregano (optional)

1 Thaw fish, if frozen. Rinse fish; pat dry with paper towels. If necessary, cut into four serving-size portions. Measure thickness of fish. Sprinkle fish with ½ teaspoon of the dried oregano and ¼ teaspoon of the pepper.

2 In a large nonstick skillet, heat oil over medium heat. Add fish, seasoned side down, and cook for 2 minutes, turning once. Add the remaining ½ teaspoon dried oregano, the remaining ¼ teaspoon pepper, tomatoes, onion, olives, wine, capers, and garlic.

3 Bring to boiling; reduce heat. Simmer, covered, for 4 to 6 minutes per ½-inch thickness of fish or until fish flakes easily when tested with a fork. Using a slotted spatula, transfer fish to shallow bowls or a serving platter; cover and keep warm.

4 For sauce, bring tomato mixture to boiling. Cook, uncovered, for 1½ to 2 minutes or until slightly thickened. Spoon sauce over fish. If desired, sprinkle with fresh oregano.

Nutrition facts per serving: 152 cal., 6 g total fat (1 g sat. fat), 23 mg chol., 211 mg sodium, 5 g carb., 18 g protein.

desserts

Chocolate-Espresso Tiramisu,
page 227

zuppa INGLESE

This is the Italian version of a trifle. The standout dessert layers custard with syrup, pound cake, and fresh raspberries and tops it off with whipped cream and chocolate curls.

Prep: 1 hour
Chill: 5 to 6 hours
Cool: 2 hours
Makes: 8 servings

⅓ **cup sugar**

1 **tablespoon cornstarch**

⅛ **teaspoon salt**

1 **cup milk**

2 **egg yolks, lightly beaten**

⅓ **cup Marsala, cream sherry, or orange juice**

⅓ **cup water**

¼ **cup sugar**

2 **tablespoons orange liqueur or orange juice**

1 **cup whipping cream**

1 **10.75-ounce frozen loaf pound cake, thawed and cut into ⅓-inch-thick slices**

3 **cups fresh raspberries**

1 **tablespoon sugar**

Chocolate shavings

Fresh raspberries (optional)

1 For custard, in a medium saucepan, stir together the ⅓ cup sugar, the cornstarch, and salt. Stir in milk. Cook and stir until thickened and bubbly. Cook and stir for 2 minutes more. Gradually stir half of the hot milk mixture into egg yolks; return to remaining hot mixture in saucepan. Cook and stir until bubbly. Cook and stir for 2 minutes more. Remove from heat. Stir in Marsala, sherry, or orange juice. Transfer to a medium bowl; cover surface with plastic wrap and chill for about 2 hours, without stirring, until completely cooled.

2 Meanwhile, for syrup, in a small saucepan, combine the water and the ¼ cup sugar. Bring to boiling over medium heat, stirring to dissolve sugar. Boil for 1 minute. Remove from heat; stir in orange liqueur or orange juice. Cool.

3 In a chilled small mixing bowl with chilled beaters, beat ½ cup of the whipping cream on medium speed with an electric mixer until soft peaks form. Gently fold whipped cream into cooled custard.

4 To assemble, in the bottom of a 2-quart soufflé dish or trifle dish, arrange about one-third of the cake slices, cutting to fit as necessary. Drizzle with about one-third of the syrup. Spoon about half of the custard over cake; sprinkle with half of the raspberries. Repeat cake, syrup, custard, and raspberry layers. Top with remaining cake slices and drizzle with remaining syrup. Cover and chill for 3 to 4 hours.

5 Just before serving, beat remaining ½ cup whipping cream and the 1 tablespoon sugar on medium speed with an electric mixer until soft peaks form. Spoon whipped cream over cake layer. Sprinkle with chocolate shavings and, if desired, additional raspberries.

Nutrition facts per serving: 390 cal., 21 g total fat (12 g sat. fat), 179 mg chol., 216 mg sodium, 45 g carb., 5 g protein.

sweet PLUM CUSTARD CAKE

Plums take the spotlight in this irresistible cake that will remind you of a custardy fruit clafouti. It's the perfect sweet addition to Sunday brunch.

Prep: 25 minutes
Bake: 50 minutes
Cool: 15 minutes
Oven: 375°F
Makes: 8 servings

 3 **eggs**
⅔ **cup whipping cream**
⅓ **cup all-purpose flour**
⅓ **cup milk**
¼ **cup granulated sugar**
 2 **tablespoons butter, melted**
 2 **teaspoons vanilla**
 2 **teaspoons finely shredded lemon peel**
⅛ **teaspoon salt**
2½ **cups thinly sliced plums and/or pears**
 2 **tablespoons granulated sugar**
 Powdered sugar (optional)
 Sweetened whipped cream (optional)

1 Preheat oven to 375°F. Generously butter the bottom and side of a 9-inch pie pan or plate; set aside.

2 In a medium bowl, combine eggs, cream, flour, milk, ¼ cup granulated sugar, melted butter, vanilla, 1 teaspoon of the lemon peel, and the salt. Beat with an electric mixer on low speed until smooth.

3 Pour about half of the batter into the prepared pan, spreading evenly. Top with plums and/or pears. Sprinkle with the remaining 1 teaspoon lemon peel. Carefully pour the remaining batter over fruit. Sprinkle with 2 tablespoons granulated sugar.

4 Bake for 50 to 55 minutes or until puffed and lightly browned. Cool in pan on a wire rack for 15 minutes (cake will fall as it cools). Serve warm. If desired, sprinkle lightly with powdered sugar and serve with sweetened whipped cream.

Nutrition facts per serving: 209 cal., 13 g total fat (7 g sat. fat), 115 mg chol., 95 mg sodium, 21 g carb., 4 g protein.

sweet VANILLA POLENTA PUDDING

Prep: 35 minutes
Stand: 20 minutes
Makes: 6 servings

2 cups fat-free milk

½ of a vanilla bean, split lengthwise

⅛ teaspoon salt

½ cup quick-cooking polenta

¼ to ⅓ cup sugar

¼ cup mascarpone cheese, softened

1 tablespoon honey

¼ cup apricot preserves or your favorite flavor of preserves

1 In a medium saucepan, combine milk, vanilla bean, and salt. Bring to simmering. Cover and remove from heat. Let stand for 15 minutes to allow the vanilla bean to infuse the milk with its flavor. Remove vanilla bean; set bean aside.

2 Bring milk mixture just to boiling over medium-high heat; reduce heat to medium. Gradually add polenta, stirring constantly. Cook and stir for 5 to 7 minutes or until mixture is very thick. Remove from heat. Stir in sugar. Let stand, covered, for 5 minutes.

3 Meanwhile, in a small bowl, combine mascarpone cheese and honey. Using the tip of a sharp knife, scrape out seeds from vanilla bean. Discard vanilla pod or reserve for another use. Stir vanilla seeds into the mascarpone mixture.

4 To serve, divide polenta among six dessert dishes. Top each with a spoonful of apricot preserves and a spoonful of mascarpone mixture. Serve warm.

Nutrition facts per serving: 212 cal., 2 g total fat (1 g sat. fat), 8 mg chol., 90 mg sodium, 43 g carb., 6 g protein.

chocolate-espresso
TIRAMISU

Prep: 50 minutes
Bake: 15 minutes
Cool: 1 hour
Chill: 6 to 24 hours
Oven: 350°F
Makes: 12 servings

24 ladyfingers, split

¼ **cup freshly brewed strong espresso**

2 **tablespoons coffee liqueur (optional)**

3 **ounces bittersweet chocolate, chopped**

1 **8-ounce carton mascarpone cheese**

1 **cup whipping or heavy cream**

¼ **cup powdered sugar**

1 **teaspoon vanilla**

2 **tablespoons coffee liqueur or freshly brewed strong espresso**

Bittersweet or semisweet chocolate, melted (optional)

Chocolate-covered coffee beans, whole or chopped (optional)

1 Layer half of the ladyfingers in a 2-quart baking dish, cutting ladyfingers to fit as necessary. Drizzle 2 tablespoons of the espresso and, if desired, 1 tablespoon of the coffee liqueur over the lady fingers. Set aside.

2 Place bittersweet chocolate in a small microwave-safe bowl. Microwave, uncovered, on 50 percent power (medium) for about 1 minute or until chocolate is melted and smooth, stirring after every 15 seconds. Set aside to cool.

3 In a large bowl, beat the mascarpone cheese, whipping cream, powdered sugar, and vanilla with an electric mixer on medium speed until soft peaks form (tips curl). Beat in the 2 tablespoons coffee liqueur or espresso and cooled chocolate until just combined.

4 Spoon half of the mascarpone mixture over cake or ladyfingers in baking dish, spreading evenly. Top with the remaining ladyfingers, cutting to fit as necessary. Drizzle with the remaining 2 tablespoons espresso and, if desired, the remaining 1 tablespoon coffee liqueur. Top with the remaining mascarpone mixture, spreading evenly.

5 Cover and chill for 6 to 24 hours. If desired, garnish with melted chocolate and chocolate-covered coffee beans.

Nutrition facts per serving: 345 cal., 22 g total fat (13 g sat. fat), 93 mg chol., 127 mg sodium, 35 g carb., 7 g protein.

sicilian TANGERINES

Start to Finish: 30 minutes
Makes: 6 servings

6 large tangerines

1 cup powdered sugar

¾ cup blanched almonds, toasted and finely ground

1¼ cups whipping cream

1 tablespoon Grand Marnier or other orange liqueur

Toasted slivered almonds (optional)

Small fresh mint leaves (optional)

1 Using a sharp knife, cut off the top one-fourth of each tangerine. If necessary, cut off a very thin slice from the bottom of each tangerine so it will stand up without rolling.

2 Using a grapefruit spoon, carefully remove the pulp from tangerines. Invert hollowed-out tangerines onto paper towels. Chop enough of the tangerine pulp to make ¾ cup. If desired, chop the remaining pulp for garnish; set aside.

3 In a small bowl, combine powdered sugar and the ground almonds.

4 In a medium bowl, combine whipping cream and Grand Marnier. Beat with an electric mixer on medium to high speed until stiff peaks form (tips stand straight). Gently fold in powdered sugar mixture. Transfer mixture to a large decorating bag fitted with a large open star tip.

5 Divide the ¾ cup chopped tangerine pulp among tangerine shells. Pipe whipped cream mixture onto tops of tangerines. If desired, chill for up to 2 hours.

6 If desired, garnish with the slivered almonds, mint leaves, and the additional chopped tangerine pulp.

Nutrition facts per serving: 368 cal., 25 g total fat (12 g sat. fat), 69 mg chol., 21 mg sodium, 36 g carb., 4 g protein.

hazelnut CREAM CASSATA

Prep: 30 minutes
Bake: 15 minutes
Cool: 10 minutes
Chill: up to 24 hours
Oven: 350°F
Makes: 12 servings

1 package 2-layer-size
  white cake mix

4 teaspoons finely
  shredded lemon peel

⅓ cup chocolate-hazelnut
  spread

⅓ cup ricotta cheese

⅓ cup seedless red
  raspberry jam

1½ cups whipping cream

2 tablespoons powdered
  sugar

⅓ cup chopped toasted
  hazelnuts (filberts)

1 tablespoon finely
  shredded lemon peel

❶ Preheat oven to 350°F. Grease and lightly flour three 9x1½-inch round cake pans. Prepare cake mix according to package directions, except stir the 4 teaspoons lemon peel into batter. Spread batter in the prepared cake pans. (If you have only two 9-inch cake pans, cover and chill one-third of the batter and bake it after the other layers have been removed from pans.) Bake for about 15 minutes or until tops spring back when lightly touched. Cool cake layers in pans on wire racks for 10 minutes. Remove layers from pans. Cool completely on wire racks.

❷ For filling: In a small bowl, combine chocolate-hazelnut spread and ricotta cheese.

❸ To assemble, place one cake layer on a serving plate. Spread with half of the jam, spreading to within ½ inch of the edge. Spread half of the filling over jam. Top with the second cake layer; spread with the remaining jam and the remaining filling. Top with the third cake layer.

❹ In a large bowl, combine whipping cream and powdered sugar. Beat with an electric mixer on medium speed just until stiff peaks form (tips stand straight). Spread top and side of cake with the whipped cream. If desired, cover loosely and chill for up to 24 hours.

❺ Before serving, in a small bowl, stir together hazelnuts and the 1 tablespoon lemon peel. Sprinkle hazelnut mixture over top of cake.

Nutrition facts per serving: 474 cal., 26 g total fat (10 g sat. fat), 45 mg chol., 367 mg sodium, 54 g carb., 5 g protein.

cannoli COOKIE STACKS

Prep: 2¾ hours
Bake: 8 minutes per batch
Oven: 375°F
Makes: about 18 cookie stacks

- 1 **15-ounce container ricotta cheese**
- 1¼ **cups all-purpose flour**
- ½ **cup ground pistachio nuts**
- ¼ **cup granulated sugar**
- ¼ **cup packed brown sugar**
- ½ **cup butter**
- 5 **ounces semisweet chocolate, chopped**
- 1 **tablespoon shortening**
  Finely chopped pistachio nuts (optional)
- ¾ **cup sifted powdered sugar**
- 1 **teaspoon vanilla**
- 2 **ounces semisweet chocolate, chopped**
- 3 **tablespoons finely chopped pistachio nuts**
- 1 **tablespoon finely chopped candied orange peel**
  Powdered sugar

1 Line a large fine-mesh sieve with a double thickness of 100% cotton cheesecloth. Set sieve over a bowl and add ricotta cheese to sieve. Cover and place in the refrigerator overnight. Discard liquid in bowl.

2 Preheat oven to 375°F. In a medium bowl, combine flour, ground nuts, granulated sugar, and brown sugar. Using a pastry blender, cut in butter until mixture resembles fine crumbs. Using your hands, work dough in bowl until it forms a ball.

3 On a lightly floured surface, roll dough to ⅛-inch thickness. Using a 2½-inch round cookie cutter, cut dough into circles, rerolling scraps as necessary (you should have 36 to 40 circles). Place circles 1 inch apart on ungreased cookie sheets.

4 Bake for about 8 minutes or until lightly browned. Transfer cookies to a wire rack and let cool.

5 In a small heavy saucepan, melt 5 ounces semisweet chocolate with shortening over low heat, stirring occasionally. Remove from heat. Spread or drizzle some of the melted chocolate on the top of each cookie. Sprinkle half of the cookies with finely chopped pistachio nuts, if desired. Place cookies, chocolate side up, on wire racks or waxed paper to let chocolate set. Drizzle any leftover chocolate on dessert plates. Set aside to let chocolate dry.

6 Meanwhile, for filling, in a medium bowl, combine drained ricotta cheese, ¾ cup powdered sugar, and vanilla. Beat with an electric mixer on medium speed until well combined. Stir in 2 ounces chocolate, 3 tablespoons finely chopped pistachio nuts, and candied orange peel. Cover and chill until ready to use, if necessary.

7 To assemble each cookie stack, place a cookie round (without nuts, if using), chocolate side up, in the center of a chocolate-drizzled dessert plate. Spoon about 2 tablespoons of the ricotta mixture on top of the cookie round. Top with another cookie round, chocolate side up. Sift powdered sugar over cookies.

Nutrition facts per serving: 248 cal., 15 g total fat (8 g sat. fat), 27 mg chol., 25 g carb., 5 g protein.

bananas FOSTER GELATO

Dig your spoon into this dense and creamy gelato for a rich caramel-banana combo unlike any other.

Prep: 30 minutes
Freeze: per manufacturer's directions
Makes: 8 servings

5 **egg yolks**

⅔ **cup packed brown sugar**

¼ **teaspoon ground cinnamon**

1¾ **cups whole milk**

¼ **cup whipping cream**

½ **teaspoon salt**

2 **ripe bananas**

1 **teaspoon lemon juice**

2 **tablespoons dark rum, or ½ teaspoon rum extract**

1 **teaspoon vanilla**

Sliced bananas (optional)

Caramel ice cream topping (optional)

1 In a medium bowl, combine egg yolks, brown sugar, and cinnamon. Beat with an electric mixer on medium speed for 4 minutes.

2 In a medium saucepan, combine milk, cream, and salt. Cook and stir just until simmering. Gradually stir about 1 cup of the hot mixture into egg yolk mixture. Return egg yolk mixture to saucepan. Cook and stir until mixture is thickened (do not boil). Place pan in a large bowl of ice water and stir for 2 to 3 minutes or until mixture is cool.

3 In a medium bowl, mash whole bananas with lemon juice; stir into egg yolk mixture. Stir in rum and vanilla (mixture may appear slightly curdled). Transfer to a large bowl. Cover and chill overnight.

4 Transfer mixture to a 1½- or 2-quart ice cream freezer. Freeze according to the manufacturer's directions. If desired, serve with sliced bananas and caramel topping.

Nutrition facts per serving: 198 cal., 7 g total fat (4 g sat. fat), 147 mg chol., 180 mg sodium, 28 g carb., 4 g protein.

metric information

The charts on this page provide a guide for converting measurements from the U.S. customary system, which is used throughout this book, to the metric system.

PRODUCT DIFFERENCES

Most of the ingredients called for in the recipes in this book are available in most countries. However, some are known by different names. Here are some common American ingredients and their possible counterparts:

- Sugar (white) is granulated, fine granulated, or castor sugar.
- Powdered sugar is icing sugar.
- All-purpose flour is enriched, bleached, or unbleached white household flour. When self-rising flour is used in place of all-purpose flour in a recipe that calls for leavening, omit the leavening agent (baking soda or baking powder) and salt.
- Light-colored corn syrup is golden syrup.
- Cornstarch is cornflour.
- Baking soda is bicarbonate of soda.
- Vanilla or vanilla extract is vanilla essence.
- Green, red, or yellow sweet peppers are capsicums or bell peppers.
- Golden raisins are sultanas.

VOLUME AND WEIGHT

The United States traditionally uses cup measures for liquid and solid ingredients. The chart, top right, shows the approximate imperial and metric equivalents. If you are accustomed to weighing solid ingredients, the following approximate equivalents will be helpful.

- 1 cup butter, castor sugar, or rice = 8 ounces = ½ pound = 250 grams
- 1 cup flour = 4 ounces = ¼ pound = 125 grams
- 1 cup icing sugar = 5 ounces = 150 grams

Canadian and U.S. volume for a cup measure is 8 fluid ounces (237 ml), but the standard metric equivalent is 250 ml.

1 British imperial cup is 10 fluid ounces.

In Australia, 1 tablespoon equals 20 ml, and there are 4 teaspoons in the Australian tablespoon.

Spoon measures are used for smaller amounts of ingredients. Although the size of the tablespoon varies slightly in different countries, for practical purposes and for recipes in this book, a straight substitution is all that's necessary. Measurements made using cups or spoons always should be level unless stated otherwise.

COMMON WEIGHT RANGE REPLACEMENTS

Imperial / U.S.	Metric
½ ounce	15 g
1 ounce	25 g or 30 g
4 ounces (¼ pound)	115 g or 125 g
8 ounces (½ pound)	225 g or 250 g
16 ounces (1 pound)	450 g or 500 g
1¼ pounds	625 g
1½ pounds	750 g
2 pounds or 2¼ pounds	1,000 g or 1 Kg

OVEN TEMPERATURE EQUIVALENTS

Fahrenheit Setting	Celsius Setting*	Gas Setting
300°F	150°C	Gas Mark 2 (very low)
325°F	160°C	Gas Mark 3 (low)
350°F	180°C	Gas Mark 4 (moderate)
375°F	190°C	Gas Mark 5 (moderate)
400°F	200°C	Gas Mark 6 (hot)
425°F	220°C	Gas Mark 7 (hot)
450°F	230°C	Gas Mark 8 (very hot)
475°F	240°C	Gas Mark 9 (very hot)
500°F	260°C	Gas Mark 10 (extremely hot)
Broil	Broil	Grill

*Electric and gas ovens may be calibrated using Celsius. However, for an electric oven, increase Celsius setting 10 to 20 degrees when cooking above 160°C. For convection or forced air ovens (gas or electric) lower the temperature setting 25°F/10°C when cooking at all heat levels.

BAKING PAN SIZES

Imperial / U.S.	Metric
9×1½-inch round cake pan	22- or 23×4-cm (1.5 L)
9×1½-inch pie plate	22- or 23×4-cm (1 L)
8×8×2-inch square cake pan	20×5-cm (2 L)
9×9×2-inch square cake pan	22- or 23×4.5-cm (2.5 L)
11×7×1½-inch baking pan	28×17×4-cm (2 L)
2-quart rectangular baking pan	30×19×4.5-cm (3 L)
13×9×2-inch baking pan	34×22×4.5-cm (3.5 L)
15×10×1-inch jelly roll pan	40×25×2-cm
9×5×3-inch loaf pan	23×13×8-cm (2 L)
2-quart casserole	2 L

U.S. / STANDARD METRIC EQUIVALENTS

⅛ teaspoon = 0.5 ml	⅓ cup = 3 fluid ounces = 75 ml
¼ teaspoon = 1 ml	½ cup = 4 fluid ounces = 125 ml
½ teaspoon = 2 ml	⅔ cup = 5 fluid ounces = 150 ml
1 teaspoon = 5 ml	¾ cup = 6 fluid ounces = 175 ml
1 tablespoon = 15 ml	1 cup = 8 fluid ounces = 250 ml
2 tablespoons = 25 ml	2 cups = 1 pint = 500 ml
¼ cup = 2 fluid ounces = 50 ml	1 quart = 1 liter

index

Note: Page references in *italics* refer to photographs.